# WAR IN THE BALKANS 1991-1993

Eric MICHELETTI and Yves DEBAY
Translated by Jean-Pierre VILLAUME

## HISTOIRE & COLLECTIONS

ISBN : *2 908 182 211*
Histoire et Collections , P.O. Box 327, Poole,Dorset BH15 2RG UK

CONTENTS

# WAR IN SLOVENIA

# WAR IN CROATIA

# WAR IN BOSNIA

# WAR IN TH

War began at 5am on 27 June 1991 when tanks and armoured vehicles of the Yugoslav People's Army roared out of their barracks, in the vicinity of Ljubljana, to oppose the breakaway of Slovenia which had just declared its independence. Few 'Southern Slavs' realised then that the days of the Yugoslav Federation were numbered.

Soon, the Slovenian, Croatian, Serbian and Macedonian federation - Yugoslavia, cobbled together in the ashes of World War 1 and cemented in blood by Tito after World War 2 - would fall apart in a storm of hatred and destruction.

When Tito died in 1980, the Yugoslav Federation began to disintegrate as political leaders became more concerned with fanning the nationalist claims of each republic rather than curing the economic woes caused by several decades of socialist mismanagement.

When the crisis started, few Western leaders realised that it was more than the breakdown of communism, and just how deeply-rooted many of the problems were. Whether out of cowardice or shortsightedness, they stood idle while the Yugoslav Federation sank deeper and deeper into war.

Nationalism soon gave way to unbridled ethnic, territorial and religious claims in Croatia and Bosnia Herzegovina, and it may realistically be feared that in years to come, the same process will repeat itself in Kosovo and Macedonia.

But the origins of today's conflict can also be traced to more ancient times. The Southern Slavs settled the region during the 6th century, and soon split into two groups. The Croatian-Slovenian group was evangelised by Rome in Latin, while the Serbs were converted to the orthodox religion by the Byzantines who taught them in Slavonic. Oddly, both ethnic groups settled on either side of what use to mark the border between the western and eastern parts of the Roman Empire.

Enjoying relative autonomy, the Croatian-Slovenes became allied to the Magyar kings (present-day Hungary), prior to

being ruled by the Holy Roman Empire and its successor, the Austrian Habsburg family. But the Serbs were not so fortunate: defeated by the Turks at the battle of Kosovo Polje in 1389, they suffered for 500 years under the Ottoman yoke.

Many migrated to the safer confines of Croatia where they became farmer-soldiers and served in the Habsburg army against the Turks. Today's Serbian minorities in Croatia are their descendants.

In the 19th century, when Turkey was known as the 'Sick Man of Europe', the Serbs were urged by the Russians to overthrow Ottoman rule. But other nations greedily ogled Tur-

# BALKANS

kish possessions, such as the Austro-Hungarian Empire which invaded and took Bosnia in 1878. From then on, independent Serbia - allied to the Czars - opposed German hegemony in the Balkans. On 28 June 1914, the murder of Arch-

duke Franz Ferdinand by Serbian student Princip triggered off World War 1. After resisting heroically and living through a terrible retreat, Serbian King Peter I was defeated by the Germans, but when the war was over, the Serbs were among the victors and modern Yugoslavia came into being with the Neuilly Treaty (1919), the Saint-Germain Treaty (1919) and the Trianon Treaty (1920) which defined the borders of the new state.

Officially known as Yugoslavia from 1929, the new nation comprised Serbia and included possessions of the former Austro-Hungarian Empire. This imposed reunification meant that the southern Slavs were forced to live under the iron rule of Serbian King Alexander who hardly left any autonomy to Croats and Slovenes.

In the 1920s, blood was shed again when Croatian representatives were shot during a parliamentary session in Belgrade. In those days, secret societies were rife, one of them being Ante Pavelic's Croatian nationalist movement. In 1934, members of that movement murdered King Alexander during a visit to Marseilles.

In 1941, it only took a few days for Germany and its allies to crush the Royal Yugoslav Army. The Nazi troops were acclaimed by the populace when they marched into Zagreb. Croatia became a satellite of the Third Reich, while Serbia lived through a severe occupation. Tito, a communist Croat, organised underground forces and was soon regarded by the Allies as Yugoslavia's leader after he had eliminated the Serbian Chetniks and the royalist soldiers opposed to both the Croatian Ustashis and his own supporters.

The country was torn by civil war. There were terror raids by Ustashis and reprisals by red partisans. After victory, Tito created a new state that soon broke away from the Soviet bloc and became an example to non-aligned countries. Making the most of the famous proverb 'divide and rule', Tito favoured the Croats while creating a Serb-controlled state, granted Bosnia's Muslims their own nationality, and conceded a specific status to Macedonians.

When Tito died in the 1980s, there was no leader who could take over from him, and this ethnic mixture could not last. Tito's 'apparatchiks' soon turned into fierce nationalists, opening yet another bloody chapter in the already complicated and tumultuous history of the Balkans.

5

# SLOVENIA'S U

At Ljubljana, on 25 June 1991, Slovenia's parliament pronounced itself overwhelmingly in favour of independence and the Republic broke away from the Yugoslav Federation.

The Slovenes have long been exposed to Austrian influence and have always felt closer to Vienna than Belgrade. Part of the Habsburg Empire since the 13th century, and traditionally wary of the Serbs, the Slovenes felt even more remote from the Federation's government and its communist ideology as they contributed 30% to Yugoslavia's gross national product. Determined not to forsake this vital source of revenue, Belgrade decided to oppose Slovenia's independence by all means - including force of arms.

Military intervention was scheduled to start at 5am on 27 June 1991.

Initially, the Federal troops planned to encircle the Slovenian capital city, then seize its airport and all border posts along the Aus-

trian border. JNA (Yugoslav People's Army) units had hardly left their barracks when Slovenian territorials (TO or Teritorialna Obramba) intervened and, in no time at all, had erected barricades and roadblocks all around the country.

Slovenian President Milan Kucan called on *'all citizens, officers and soldiers to resist the aggression against the Slovenian people'.* Belgrade answered with an ultimatum stating that all 'resistance to the Federal forces will be broken'.

On the border, clashes took place with guards when heliborne and airborne operations were conducted with armoured support. The JNA seized about a dozen border posts, but 15 remained under Slovenian control. Fighting was fierce and, by the morning of 28 June, the situation was still extremely confused. JNA armoured reinforcements attempted to cross in from Croatia but were repelled.

# ISING

In Slovenia, the Federal troops' situation became more and more desperate. Badly led and poorly planned, the military operations failed. Most JNA barracks were soon surrounded by tough Slovenian territorials. Federal officers were no longer able to cope, and many non-Serbian-born conscripts chose to desert and returned home. Slovenian independence had been achieved easily, in less than a week, and was recognised six months later by the international community.

The JNA had paid a heavy price and could no longer be regarded as a national army embracing all Yugoslavia's constituent nationalities.

Humiliated after its failure, it all but broke up, and soon became solely Serbia's army, serving one people only.

Over the next few months,the Croats would have the opportunity to get better acquainted with the JNA.

# LJUBLJANA BESIEG

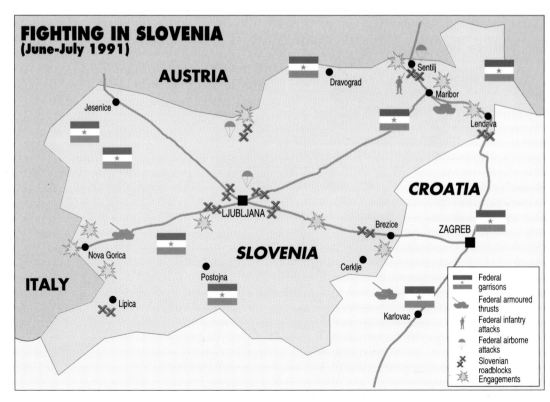

**FIGHTING IN SLOVENIA**
**(June-July 1991)**

AUSTRIA

Jesenice

Dravograd

Sentilj

Maribor

Lendava

CROATIA

LJUBLJANA

Brezice

ZAGREB

Nova Gorica

SLOVENIA

Cerklje

ITALY

Postojna

Lipica

Karlovac

| | Federal garrisons |
| --- | --- |
| | Federal armoured thrusts |
| | Federal infantry attacks |
| | Federal airborne attacks |
| | Slovenian roadblocks |
| | Engagements |

*Above right.*
**Slovenian policemen of an anti-terrorist unit in a Ljubljana suburb. They are ready to bar the way to the JNA vehicles positioned on the international airport. But the Federal troops at this strategic site did not make a move.**

*Right.*
*Persistent rumours of impending air raids against the Presidential building and armoured attacks by the JNA caused tension and anxiety in the Slovenian capital. The Slovenian guards on duty at the Presidential building were on permanent alert.*

As soon as the Slovenes decided to go it alone on 25 June 1991, Ljubljana, Slovenia's capital city, was put under a state of emergency and prepared for a siege.

Manned by policemen and Presidential guard soldiers, roadblocks and barricades were set up around the parliament building and government house. BOV vehicles in Slovenian police colours patrolled the city and, in the days that followed, sirens sounded several air raid warnings.

A JNA Gazelle helicopter was shot down with light weapons.

War had started in what used to be Yugoslavia.

*Above.*
*At the Nova Gorica border post, near the Italian border, Slovenian territorials wait for further orders after repelling a Federal onslaught. In a matter of minutes, the Slovenes had knocked out two T-55s, and captured four T-54s and one engineer T-55.*

*Right.*
*After hearing their President urging them to fight for their independence, Slovenian territorials took up arms to defend their homeland - as the JNA stood by powerless.*

*Far right.*
*In northern Slovenia, near the Austrian border, a Slovenian territorial trains his RBR-80 anti-tank rocket launcher on buildings converted into strongholds by the Federals. For the JNA however, the situation was already hopeless.*

# COMBAT IN SLOVENIA

Two days after Slovenia proclaimed independence, on the night of 27-28 June, several Slovenian civilians and one policeman were shot dead. The murderers who had opened fire from an unmarked car were never identified

The next day, JNA heliborne and armoured units left their barracks to seize Ljubljana airport and border posts to isolate Slovenia from neighbouring Italy and Austria. Carried out by Serbian, Slovenian, Croatian, Bosnian and Macedonian conscripts, these operations were badly co-ordinated and often failed disastrously.

JNA columns found themselves held up by truck blockades and incapable of manoeuvring. After short but violent fights, the Federal forces were neutralised by Slovenes whose motivation and courage more than made up for their lack of heavy armament.

# SLOVENIAN TERR
# DEFEND THEIR H

DUTY FREE SHOP

*Right.*
*On 29 June 1991, Slovenes captured several T-54 MBTs at the Setilji border post, near Austria. The tanks were then turned against a company of JNA diehards entrenched in a mountain stronghold overlooking the border. Two days later, the Federals surrendered to the Slovenes after a spirited last stand.*

*Below.*
*Painting the insignia of territorial forces on the turret of a T-54 MBT captured from the JNA.*

*Above.*
*In this engagement, the Slovenes captured about a dozen tanks and armoured vehicles from the Federal forces. In no time, they turned them against their erstwhile owners. Slovenes are seen here replenishing the ammunition stores of one of the T-54s captured in Sentilji.*

Military experts used to regard Yugoslavia's army as the fourth most powerful force in Europe, even though large discrepancies and doubts existed about its actual strength. Obsessed by fears of a Soviet takeover, Marshal Tito, himself a former partisan, created territorial armies (TO or Teritorialna Obramba) to deter any aggressive move by the Russians.

At a time of conflict, TO reservists would have been called up and sent to take control of strategic points. The TO had heavy weapons, but they were of older and inferior design to those of the JNA. In wartime, the TO would also supply men and equipment to underground fighters operating behind enemy lines. Each republic had its own territorial army. Later, these would spawn the armies of Slovenia, Croatia and Bosnia.

In Slovenia, TO plain-clothed militiamen were up to their task, but instead of facing the external threat Tito had anticipated, their enemies came from within Yugoslavia itself.

*Right.*
*On 1 July, at the Jezersko border post, Slovenes only just repelled JNA soldiers back into the mountains. Before withdrawing, the Federals unleashed a volley of 30mm shells from the twin guns of their self-propelled anti-aircraft vehicles, like the one shown in the background.*

*Far right.*
*Two Slovenian territorials posing in front of the Sentilji border post they have just captured from JNA units. Thinking that a Slovenian uprising was impossible, JNA Command was caught unawares and soon proved unable to cope with the situation. Outmanoeuvred and disappointed by the poor showing of its troops, JNA Command had no alternative but to agree to a ceasefire.*

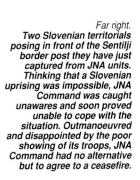

*Right and below*
**Late June 1991.**
Overestimating its power, a JNA armoured convoy ventured into Slovenian territory without infantry support. The column was beaten in less than two minutes with the Federal Army losing two M-60 APCs and one M-84 MBT. The Slovenes vanished after striking. This short but deadly engagement also cost the JNA about 10 men.

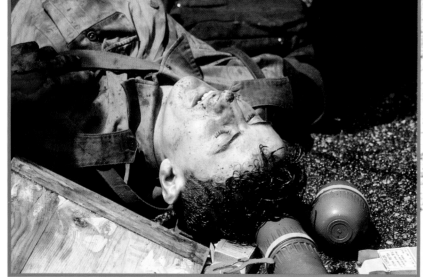

# AMBUS

# OF A JNA CONVOY

On 3 July 1991, Federal armoured columns left their barracks in Jastrebarsko and Rijeka (in Croatia), for Slovenia where Federal troops were in dire need of support. A squadron of M-84 and T-55 MBTs protecting M-60 and M-80 APCs set off for Brezice in Slovenia in order to secure a nuclear plant. After crossing into Slovenian territory, the column was ambushed. The Slovenians destroyed two M-60s and one M-84. The rest of the columm was ordered to withdraw. This was the last time the JNA intervened in Slovenia.

In less than a week, the ceasefire agreement was signed and Slovenia's independence was obtained without further bloodshed.

However, a storm was brewing in neighbouring Croatia which had also just proclaimed its independence.

# THE AGONY OF A FEDERAL CONVOY

On 1 July 1991, a column of 12 BOV-3 anti-aircraft vehicles armed with triple 20mm guns was ordered out of its Ljubljana barracks. The Federal troops were tasked with recovering any stray military equipment lest it fell into Slovenian hands. The column was coasting along the Ljubljana-Zagreb road when 5th Army Command ordered it to head for the Croatian border and join up with an armoured squadron coming in from Zagreb. Most of the Slovenian conscripts had already deserted and many Serbian officers were only too eager to leave the Slovenian Republic where their presence was no longer wanted. The column was in radio contact with headquarters and the first part of the journey, some 65km, was covered without incident. After a night's bivouac, the column drove off and the officers become optimistic when the armored vehicles rumbled through the vil-

lage of Toplice: the Croatian border and the JNA tanks were only a short distance away.

The BOVs advanced in groups of three, separated by a distance of 30m. Suddenly, as it was going through a forest, the convoy ran into a road block of trucks. From well concealed positions along the roadside, Slovenian territorials opened up on the BOV 3s and blasted the vehicles with B-10 recoilless guns, Armbrust anti-tank rockets and rifle grenades.

Almost immediately, one of the BOVs was hit by a rocket and burst into flames. Then another was hit by a rifle grenade which exploded in the engine bay, killing the driver and showering the rest of the crew with splinters. A third vehicle was also hit and burnt fiercely, but its crew was luckier and escaped from the blazing wreck. The JNA troops were quick to react and the surviving BOV-3s swung into top

*Below.*
*A column of BOV-3 self-propelled anti-aircraft vehicles has just been ambushed by Slovenian territorials. One of the vehicles has been hit but the Federal troops somehow repelled the attackers. After assessing their losses, the Federal soldiers organised their defence.*

gear and swept the edge of the forest with their 20mm cannon, firing 750 rounds a minute. Wearing helmets adorned with red stars, several infantrymen followed up by jumping out of the vehicles and, attacking on foot, captured two Slovenes and several B-10 guns. But the rest of the territorials had taken to their heels and vanished into the forest. The Slovenes had the last laugh too: when they tried to clear the road, the Federal soldiers found the steering wheels of the trucks jammed. The Federals had been beaten, and this first ambush cost them three vehicles and four men. Journalists who were covering the event assisted with the evacuation of two badly wounded soldiers.

The commander of the convoy requested air assistance and in no time, two Jastreb and two MiG-21 fighter-bombers had reduced the truck blockade to smithereens. The way was now clear and the convoy proceeded, occasionally loosing off random bursts of fire at the surrounding forest, until it reached a stretch of open road where it could settle for the night.

On 3 July at dawn, the radio announced that the column of tanks the convoy was to meet up with had been repelled. The columns never met up and, dispirited, the convoy commander gave the order to abandon the vehicles. On foot, the soldiers fell back to a nearby air base still controlled by their own forces.

In the morning, the Slovenians seized all the undamaged vehicles.

*Above.*
*Searching for Slovenian territorials, Federal soldiers advance past a blockade of trucks laid in their path to slow down their advance.*

*Left.*
*The engagement is over and the Federal soldiers take advantage of the lull in the fighting to tend their wounded before evacuating them. The Federal troops abandoned their vehicles a few hours later and withdrew under the cover of darkness.*

21

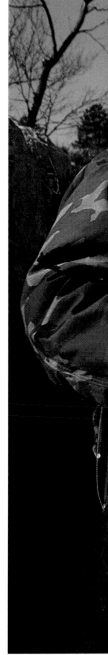

# OPPOSING

*Above left.*
**Pictured in the Bihac salient in February 1993, this Bosnian Muslim officer is armed with a 9mm UZI submachine-gun.**

*Above right.*
**A Bosnian Serbian militiaman, pictured on the heights surrounding Sarajevo in the winter of 1992-93. He is armed with an M-70 7.62mm assault rifle.**

Unlike Bosnia Herzegovina, the republics of Croatia and Slovenia did not try to keep out of the conflict: both knew that one day, they would be drawn into the war. In May 1991, the Croatian forces stood at five active and four reserve territorial brigades which had retained their former territorial defence structure.

The two republics, however, were critically short of heavy equipment. In the opening months of the conflict the only MBTs, APCs and artillery pieces they had were those captured when the JNA barracks were taken over and those handed over by

Croatian and Slovenian deserters.

But neither Slovenia nor Bosnia suffered from a shortage of volunteers.

Every Yugoslav is a potential partisan, and Tito's regime had promoted the cult of the armed civilian. When war broke out in Slovenia, more than 60,000 men, reservists or shooting club members fell in with the Slovenian Forces.

In 1991, the state of armed forces in Yugoslavia stood as follows: the JNA fielded 130,000 men (including 55,000 in Croatia and 20,000 in Slovenia); the Croatia National Guard totalled 40,000 men and

# ORCES

*Top right.*
*A JNA officer during the opening stages of the war. Unlike the conscripts, most officers and NCOs remained loyal to the Serbian government.*

*Right.*
*A Croatian National Guardsman in May 1991. He is armed with an M-70 assault rifle; in less than a year, the Croatian National Guard turned from a militia into a fully-fledged army.*

15,000 armed policemen, and the Slovenian territorial defence numbered 35,000 men and 8,000 armed policemen.

*Right.*
*On the Zagreb-Ljubljana highway, a JNA armoured column waits for the order to advance into Slovenian territory. The soldiers are still sitting in their M-60P APCs, while their officers anxiously wait for further developments. Five of their number have just been killed about 100m away.*

*Below.*
*Early in summer 1991, soldiers were still fighting in shirt-sleeve order, like this JNA officer. But a few months later, when fighting broke out in Croatia, officers were issued with bullet-proof vests, assault rifles with scopes and disposable rocket launchers*

# THE YUGOSI

In 1949, Marshal Tito broke away from his wartime allies, Stalin and Churchill. A genuine communist, Tito created the movement of non-aligned nations, gathering together countries without allegiance either to West or East. But when Red Army tanks crushed the Hungarian Uprising in 1956, Tito realised that Soviet intervention was a serious threat to Yugoslavia. To deter any aggressive move by the Soviets, Tito created a formidable army which was also meant to be the symbol of national unity. In wartime, this army would rely on its manoeuvring power to crush an enemy which had already been paralysed by TO reservists who would harrass the aggressor with guerilla attacks.

In 1991, the JNA boasted Europe's fourth largest army and its forces stood at 1,850 MBTs, 600 artillery pieces, 198 helicopters and 455 aircraft. Providing 42% of the manpower and 80% of the officers and NCOs, the Serbs constituted the JNA's largest ethnic component, followed by the Croats (14.2%), and Montenegrines (9.4%). Slovenes, Macedonians and Bosnians contributed only a small percentage to the overall establishment.

The JNA was organised into four commands: 1st in Belgrade, 3rd in Skop-

Below.
When the ceasefire was
signed on 3 July, JNA
engineers went about
clearing the ordnance and
derelict equipment strewn all
over the battlefield.

# V PEOPLE'S
# RMY

je, 5th in Zagreb and Naval Command was based in Split. The Guards Brigade was quartered in Belgrade. Each command comprised five or six infantry,
two armoured and two artillery divisions. When Croatia declared independence, the 3rd and 5th Military Commands were transferred to Banja Luka in Macedonia and Naval Command was shifted from Split to Titograd in Montenegro.

When war started in Croatia, most of the Serbian officers adhered to Tito's
doctrine and staunchly supported the concept of a Yugoslav Federation. At
least 95% of them belonged to the communist party.

In less than a week, the myth of the multi-racial army was shattered. More
than reluctant to fight, conscripts deserted in droves and joined the ranks of
the territorial forces of their own republics.

Disgruntled, the Serbian officers did the same themselves and took sides
with the Serbian Republic. This move was accelerated by purges among high
ranking officers. As the war dragged on, the red star of Yugoslavia disappea-
red from helmets and forage caps, and was replaced by the white, red and
blue cockade of Greater Serbia.

25

*Early on 2 July, an armoured column of 5th Army tried to skirt the roadblocks set up by the Slovenes on the new border between Croatia and Slovenia. Coming from Zagreb, the convoy was composed of M-84 MBTs, the most modern equipment in the JNA's inventory. A redoubtable fighting tool in open country, the M-84 didn't perform as well when deployed in urban surroundings or broken ground. At the onset of the conflict, the JNA fielded no fewer than 700 M-84s.*

# JNA'S ARMO

# RED SPEARHEAD

Armour and strong artillery support were the pillars of the JNA whereas infantry duties were entrusted to large bodies of partisans conducting guerilla attacks against invaders. This resulted in Yugoslav regulars being proficient in armour and artillery tactics but undertrained as infantrymen.

For example, during the operations in Croatia in the autumn of 1991, JNA officers used Serbian paramilitary forces as assault troops, while regulars provided support with their heavy weapons and tanks. But this weakness notwithstanding, the JNA was a formidable fighting tool fielding more than 1,800 tanks, 400 of which were M-84s, the Yugoslav-built version of the Soviet T-72. The M-84 can be distinguished from the T-72 by its double row of smoke

dischargers. It also has improved electronics (superior to the Soviet model) and a Swedish-made Bofors fire control system. Its 1,100hp, V-12 supercharged diesel engine propels it to speeds of up to 70km/h. It has well sloped armour, is very manoeuvrable, and its 125mm gun lobs HE-FRAG, HEAT-FS and APFSDS-T shells to ranges of up to 12,000m. Secondary armament includes one hull-mounted 12.7mm and one co-axial 7.62mm MG. In capable hands, the M-84 is a redoubtable tank that also proves very hard to knock out. However, a direct hit to its ammunition bay will cause the M-84 to blow up, inevitably resulting in the turret being blown away.

Surprisingly for an army versed in armour tactics, the Federals never used their heavy tanks in large formations, even though the flat country of western Slavonia is well suited for these sorts of deployments. Instead, the JNA used its tanks in penny packets and severe losses were incurred - especially when M-84s operated in urban surroundings unsupported by infantry. During the 'Barracks War' in the autumn of 1991, the Croats seized many M-84s from the Federals and recently purchased T-72s from East Germany's former Volksarmee. According to Western armour experts, any engagement in which such tanks would be pitted against each other would result in both sides suffering frightful losses.

The older T-54/55 is the mainstay ot JNA's

armoured units and, although obsolete by modern-day standards, this tank has given sterling service on the Yugoslav battleground where it was often used in the direct artillery support role. This rugged and sturdy MBT is now on strength with both sides after the Croats captured many T-55s during the 'Barracks War'.

In the spring of 1991, JNA mechanised units operated some 600 APCs, the most modern being the M-980 model, also available in its updated BVP-M80A version with French AMX engine and running gear. The M-980 is fitted with twin Sagger anti-tank missiles, and a licence-built Swiss-designed Oerlikon 20mm gun. The armament is mounted on the hull, in the same way as on the Soviet BMP-2.

With a crew of two, the M-80 can carry eight fully-equipped infantrymen. Its updated BVP-M80A version is wider, more powerful but also one tonne heavier (14t) than the standard model.

The JNA also has substantial quantities of M-60P tracked APCs, of the same generation as the American M-113, and powered by Austrian Steyr engines.

Carrying eight infantrymen, the M-60P is armed with one US M-2 12.7mm heavy machine-gun. Like the M-80, the M-60 is known as the 'Transporter' by soldiers of both sides, and it is also available in its M-60B anti-tank version, armed with two B-10 82mm recoilless guns.

In the 1970s, a series of light armoured vehicles fitted with Cadillac Gage wheels was introduced into the Yugoslav army. Known as the BOV, these vehicles are available in several versions: the BOV-1 anti-tank model armed with six Sagger missiles, the air-defence BOV-3 fitted with triple 20mm M-55 cannon, the BOV-30 with twin 30mm cannon, and the BOV-M armed with one 12.7mm heavy machine-gun. With the exception of the M-84 MBTs manufactured on the Bosnian-Croatian border, all these vehicles were built in Serbian state-owned plants. When the Serbs felt that war was looming, they transferred to their own territory all the armament and ammunition plants previously located for their larger part in Croatia and Bosnia Herzegovina.

# JUNE 1991: CROATIA'S INDEPENDENCE

*Above.*
*Silent for many years, the Croats overwhelmingly expressed their wish for independence when, in 1990, free elections were held for the first time in their republic. Croatian nationalism sprung anew, with red and white checkered flags being openly displayed.*

*Above right.*
*On 25 June 1991, President Franjo Tudjman declared Croatia's independence - on the same day as Slovenia. But unlike the Slovenes, the Croats had to fight bitterly for the right to autonomy and paid a heavy toll in human lives.*

30

When Croatia proclaimed its independence on 25 June 1991, this prosperous republic contributed 21% to Yugoslavia's national wealth. But unlike Slovenia, Croatia has no natural barriers with the rest of the country.

This republic also has strong Serbian settlements, dating back to the 16th and 17th centuries, and descended from the farmer soldiers who were encouraged by the Habsburgs to settle down in this region and guard the approaches of the Austrian Empire from the Turks in an area which became known as the frontier — in Serb 'Krajina'.

At least 12% of Croatia's population is of Serbian extraction. The Serbian minority created armed militias long before Croatia declared its independence and declared itself the 'Autonomous Serbian Republic of Krajina'. It set up a 12,000-man militia reinforced by Serbs sent in from Belgrade. Among them was 'Captain Dragan', an Australian-born Serb who soon become notorious for the numerous atrocities he commited on the local population. In other territories, the Serbs created armed militias without the Federal Army raising an eyebrow.

A climate of insecurity prevailed and on 2 May 1991, two Croatian policemen were abducted in Borovo-Selo in western Slavonia. Other policemen sent to liberate them were ambushed and 12 of them were shot.

These murders triggered off a savage war on the banks of the Danube.

*A member of Croatia's Guard of Honour, on duty in front of the Zagreb Parliament. His richly adorned uniform bears testimony to the wealth of Croatia's heritage.*

31

# THE CROATIAN

On 28 May 1991, Croatian Defence Minister, General Martin Spegelj, officially announced the creation of a Croatian National Guard. The Guard wasn't created in one day, but had secretly evolved over several years under the guise of the Croatian territorial army.

Initially, the Guard only included male and female volunteers (mobilisation wasn't decreed by President Franjo Tudjman until the autumn of 1991), and was mostly composed of police and Federal reserve forces. The officers were ex-communists formerly commissioned with the JNA. Many were not up to their task; as for subalterns, they were trained under fire.

When created, the Guard comprised nine infantry brigades (five of which were active),and each averaged from 2,500 to 3,000 men and women.

The total force amounted to 13,000 active members who could be backed up by 10,000 reservists available within 24 hours, and 19 'special intervention' companies.

But apart from several BOV-M and BTR-60 armoured vehicles loaned by the police, the

*Above.*
*Zagreb, 28 May 1991: the Croatian National Guard parading for the first time on the day it was officially created. Here are shown elements of the ground forces.*

*Right.*
*Here are a member of the navy, a force that, until January 1992, only amounted to a few patrol boats and launches.*

*Far right. A female Guard member. numerous women serve in the ranks of the Croatian National Guard.*

32

# TIONAL GUARD

Guard was critically short of heavy armament. True, there was no shortage of light weapons, such as Yugoslav, Romanian and Hungarian AK-47s and AKMs, SA-80 assault rifles, and Ultimax 100 5.56mm light machine-guns purchased in Singapore.

Guardsmen also had plentiful supplies of Czech Skorpion, MP-5 Heckler & Koch and UZI submachine-guns bought in Great Britain, and many Guardsmen were issued with Spas-12 riot guns.

As in all civil wars, fighters had to make do with whatever armament they could lay their hands on and inevitably, obsolete armament surfaced. The Guard's inventory soon included German Mauser 98K bolt action rifles, and its locally-made version, the M-48 model. Also in use were the famous Russian World War 2 PPSh-41 submachine-gun and the German MP-40 Schmeisser, as well as its local version, the MP-56.

The strange looking American MGV-176 submachine-gun with its transparent magazine is also on issue. Chambered for the .22 Long Rifle cartridge, its firing rate is 1,600

round/min. Anti-tank armament was adequate, most of it manufactured in state-owned plants, such as the VM-80s, a licence-built version of the US LAW, the M-57 (identical to the RPG-7), and the 90mm M-79, a lethal weapon comparable with the French LRAC. Also purchased abroad were Hungarian RPG-7s and German Armbrust rocket launchers (also obtained from Singapore).

For indirect fire support, the Guard had a whole range of mortars, including 50mm (V-8), 60mm (M-57) and 81mm (M-31) calibres. Some heavier 120mm pieces were also on strength.

When fighting started in the autumn of 1991, the Croats received light weapons (FAL and UZI assault rifles) from Argentina, and extra armament such as AK-47s were supplied from former East German Army stores.

But heavy armament was in short supply, and the first tanks sporting the white and red check flag didn't appear until the end of the 'Barracks War' in November 1991.

In 1991, the Guard felt it was ready. Its baptism of fire would be bloody.

**SERBIAN SETTLEMENTS IN CROATIA**

SLOVENIA

ZAGREB

Rijeka

Karlovac  Sisak  Novska

Osijek

SERBIA

CROATIA

Vukovar

Vinkovci

Banja Luka

Zadar

**BOSNIA-HERZEGOVINA**

Rnin

Mer Adriatique

SARAJEVO

Split

Dubrovnik

Areas with strong Serbian settlements

Serbian minorities

*Left.*
*In spring 1991, the only armoured vehicles the Croats had were those of the police, such as this BTR-60PB. On the battlefield, they proved no match for the heavy tanks of the JNA.*

*Above.*
*In the village of Tenja, in western Slavonia, a young Serbian volunteer on duty near the road to Osijek. He is armed with an obsolete US Thompson submachine-gun. With its population divided equally between the Serbs and the Croats, Tenja was occupied by the former throughout the summer of 1991.*

AUSTRIA

HUNGARY

SLOVENIA

ROMANIA

ZAGREB

VOJVODINA

CROATIA

Karlovac

BOSNIA-HERZEGOVINA

BELGRADE

SARAJEVO

SERBIA

BULGARIA

MONTENEGRO

Adriatic
Sea

KOSOVO

ALBANIA

MACEDONIA

GREECE

SerbiA

"Greater Serbia", comprising part of Croatia, most of Bosnia-Herzegovina, and territories annexed from Hungary and Romania

## "GREATER SERBIA"

Created as soon as the Serbian Republic of Krajina came into being, the Serbian militias evolved principally from local police forces (Serbian policemen made up 60-80% of the force in Croatian regions with strong Serbian minorities).

# THE SERBIAN

*Above right.*
**Right from the start in the fighting in Croatia, the JNA sided with the Serbs and provided them with arms and ammunition to fight Croatian police units. Pictured at Glina, this JNA M-84 was positioned outside the city, ready to open up on Croatian vehicles.**

*Right.*
**This barrier adorned with the Yugoslav national flag marked the border of Serbian-held territory in eastern Slavonia in July 1991.**

In addition to the militias of Slavonia and Bosnia, the Republic of Krajina fielded some 18,000 fighters and, as in Belgrade, numerous Serbian nationalist movements spawned militias and dispatched them to the Croatian front. These men belonged to various nationalist factions such as the Serbian Movement for Renewal, the Royalist Party, the famous Chetniks, or to smaller, lesser-known formations such as the White Eagles, Czar Lazar, Dusan the Mighty - all famous names from Serbian history.

Armament was available in sufficient quantities, and TO arms depots were placed at the Militias' disposal. Tanks, artillery, multiple rocket launchers, and even a handful of helicopters were also handed over to the Chetniks by the JNA who also supplied instructors. Well led and suitably-equipped the Serbian militias were responsible for violent incidents with the Croatian police forces. In July, they embarked on a war of conquest. 'Greater Serbia' was in the making.

But soon, Serbia's territorial ambitions gave way to a reign of terror as the Serbian militiamen with their Albanian, Russian and Romanian auxiliaries committed countless atrocities. Prisoners were systematically beaten up or tor-

Left.
*In Tenja, a Serbian fighter proudly displays a Chetnik badge on his forage cap. By autumn 1991, the Serbian militia had already become notorious around the world for the numerous atrocities they had committed in Croatia. A few months later, they would turn on the Bosnians.*

tured to death. Using the World War 2 massacres committed by Ustashis as a pretext, Serbian militias raped, killed and plundered in the name of ethnic cleansing, while the Federal Army stood by and watched.

Terror had become Greater Serbia's major weapon.

# MILITIAS

*Above.*
An authentic World War I Lewis machine-gun in position near Bjelovar. This weapon was guarding a bridge and operated by Croatian police.

*Right.*
Armed with a Czech-made ZB-26 light machine-gun, this Croatian soldier defends a trench from Serbian attackers. Of World War 2 vintage, his weapon must have been retrieved from an attic where it had been hidden since that conflict ended.

# OLD WEAPONS IN ACTION

*Above.*
**Time for a break. Belonging to HOS (Croatia's ultra nationalist faction), this militiaman is armed with a German Mauser KAR-98 rifle, an ageing but lethal weapon that still proves its worth in sniping.**

As in all civil wars, protagonists use whatever weapons they can lay their hands on, and countless World War 2 weapons have been pilfered from garrets and issued to Yugoslav fighters.

*Above.*
*Clad in East German clothing (camouflage parka and helmet), this Croat carries an M-59 submachine-gun, derived from the famous World War 2 German M-40 Schmeisser. This fighter was pictured in December 1991, on the Nova-Gradiska front, eastern Slavonia.*

*Above right.*
*Poorly clad, these Croatian volunteers were pictured near Vukovar as they defended their village with the tenacity of people with nothing left to lose. The far end of the road where they were deployed was already under Serbian control.*

*Right.*
*To get the arms and equipment they needed to defend their homeland, the Croats shopped all over Europe for surplus materiel, then smuggled it home through various borders. These 4x4 vehicles pictured in Dubica, western Slavonia, used to be on issue to Dutch forces. This ragtag equipment enabled the Croats to hold out until autumn 1991.*

# BLACK SUMMER FOR CROATIA

In May 1991, several Croatian policemen were brutally tortured and put to death in Borovo Selo, Slavonia. These murders were the first in a series of violent incidents perpetrated by Serbian militias. During the last week of June, the police station of Glina, Krajina, was set upon and wrecked. The Pakrac region, Krajina and parts of Slavonia flared up during the next month.

The tactic used by Serbs to oust the Croatian population hardly ever varied: armed gangs arrived unexpectedly and caused friction within the population. When the police or the National Guard intervened to restore order, the Fede-

*Below.*
*A National Guardsman monitoring enemy moves from Croatian front-line positions near Kostajnica. Besieged by Federal forces in September 1991, Kostajnica surrendered two months later.*

41

ral Army stepped in with tanks and APCs, and officially took control of the area. (However, supported or encouraged by JNA command, Serbian militias could move about as they wished.)

The Serbian militias received more heavy equipment as well as assistance from reservists and officers 'on the inactive list' during the Federal deployment in Slavonia. Initially, the Serbian officers wore nondescript uniforms, but soon donned JNA camouflage outfits.

Backed up and supplied by the Federal Army, the Chetniks advanced towards the coast and attempted to capture Krajina and Slavonia as a first move. Their secondary aim was to wreck Croatia's economy by splitting that republic asunder, before heading for the Adriatic Sea and providing Serbia with its long sought-after maritime outlet at Zadar.

Discreet at first, Serbian expansionist ambitions soon became blatant, but still only met with European indifference.The militias worked hand in hand with the JNA — now Federal in name only — and a tool in Serbia's hands. Serbian militiamen were carried in JNA APCs,

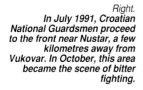

*Right.*
*In July 1991, Croatian National Guardsmen proceed to the front near Nustar, a few kilometres away from Vukovar. In October, this area became the scene of bitter fighting.*

and the Federal forces also supplied them with ammunition whenever they took over Croatian villages.

The tactic the Serbs most frequently resorted to was to send sniper teams behind the Croatian front lines where they created a climate of insecurity by opening fire at random targets. Mortars and artillery then opened up on the villages to frighten the population and finally, well armed militiamen supported by tanks rushed the villages, clearing them of their inhabitants. The Croatian menfolk were shot or detained in camps, while elderly people, women and children swelled the pitiful columns of refugees. The same methods were used in Bosnia seven months later.

Deprived of heavy armament, the Croatian National Guardsmen tried to resist but, however courageous, could only slow down the well-motivated and better-equipped Serbs.

Dozens of villages, such as Kostajnica, Jabukovac and Petrinja in northern Krajina, fell to the Serbs. Even Sisak, 60km from Zagreb was threatened. In eastern Slavonia, Vukovar and Osijek were besieged.

It was Croatia's black summer.

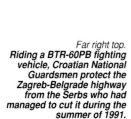

*Far right top.*
*Riding a BTR-60PB fighting vehicle, Croatian National Guardsmen protect the Zagreb-Belgrade highway from the Serbs who had managed to cut it during the summer of 1991.*

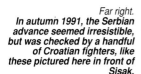

*Far right.*
*In autumn 1991, the Serbian advance seemed irresistible, but was checked by a handful of Croatian fighters, like these pictured here in front of Sisak.*

# CROATIA'S MAKESHIFT VEHICLES

The Croats used every means they could to check the Serbian onslaught - including huge, homemade, armoured vehicles. However heavy, underpowered and sluggish, these monsters were put to good use by the Croats to carry National Guardsmen to the front. Usually, they were built on a truck or bulldozer chassis, and some were armed with a machine-gun or 20mm gun.

During the 'Barracks War' in September, the Croats captured a quantity of Federal APCs, resulting in the withdrawal of these makeshift personnel carriers from the front line.

Some were later dispatched to the rear where they were used to oppose Chetnik infiltration.

About 100 such vehicles were built, and many were easy prey to Serbian militiamen's rocket launchers.

*Above.*
*These M-53/70 self-propelled guns were abandoned in the halls of the JNA's Armoured Brigade's barracks in Karlovac and captured by the Croats in December 1991.*

# THE 'BARRACK.

*Above right.*
*Croats celebrating their victory after capturing a T-55 and turning it against its former owners. The Croats had to wait until October to operate a force of about 100 tanks and armoured vehicles.*

*Far right.*
*Pictured in the suburbs of Karlovac, a T-34/85 abandoned by the JNA after an unsuccessful attempt at breaking out of the besieged barracks.*

At the end of July, Belgrade complied with the Brioni Agreements by pulling the JNA out of Slovenia. Two months of fighting in this republic had humiliated the Federal army. But Belgrade had learnt its lesson and was determined not to repeat this humbling experience in Croatia.

After the JNA had withdrawn from Slovenia, Croatian leaders feared that it would turn all its might against their republic, as the agreements had made no provision for withdrawal from Croatia, which had become independent on 25 June. Indeed the JNA had kept the right to intervene in Croatia to protect the Serbian minority there.

Feeling that Serbian militias were about to go on the offensive in Croatia, the National Guard decided to besiege the Federal barracks. Initially, the Croats cut off the water and power supplies, hoping that this would force the Federal troops to surrender or withdraw. This worked with some garrisons which capitulated without a fight, others however, made bloody attempts to break out. Some Serbian commanders shelled the city surrounding their barracks - in some cases, like in Voradzine, without considering the areas inhabited by their own families.

At Karlovac, in central Croatia, the Federal forces tried to break out: two of their tanks were destroyed but others wrought terrible havoc before returning to the barracks. Whenever the Croats felt superior, they stormed the barracks, as in Bjelovar where the Fede-

# WAR'

ral defenders fought to the last man.

To relieve the beleaguered garrisons and intimidate the Croats, the Yugoslav Air Force intervened massively but without great success and instead lost about 10 aircraft.

By 22 September, 32 barracks and military installations were in Croatian hands and, at last, the National Guardsmen had the heavy armament they needed: T-55s had been retrieved from Sibenik, M-80 APCs, BOVs and 105mm howitzers were obtained from Bjelovar.

In October, during a precarious ceasefire and under EEC observers' supervision, the undamaged barracks were evacuated and part of the armament they contained was recovered by the Serbs.

Fighting had escalated in September, evolving from armed rebellion into open warfare. The Serbian war aims were now only too clear: use the presence of a Serbian minority as a pretext to create a 'Greater Serbia' that would be home to all the Serbs. Incensed when the Croatian National Guard attacked its barracks, the JNA entered the fray and committed some 150,000 men (including militias and Chetniks), supported by 300 tanks, 700 APCs, 1,500 artillery pieces, and about 100 fighter-bombers.

The Yugoslav Navy blockaded the Croatian harbours of Split, Zadar and Rijeka to prevent the delivery of armament to the Croats.

In addition to local activities, Federal command launched three attacks: one in the south, aimed at splitting Croatia and seizing the Dalmatian harbours (and threatening Zadar, Sibenik and Gospic). A second thrust involving armoured units was launched at Karlovac to sever the

*Below.*
*In the autumn and winter of 1992, JNA T-54s were deployed on the plains of Slavonia to conquer and hold as much ground as possible. The Serbs feel that these conquests should place them in a stronger bargaining situation when peace talks are initiated .*

*Right.*
*More rugged than the M-84, the T-54 played a vital role in the battles between Serbs and Croats. After operating in their conventional role in the short autumn 1991 campaign, the tanks dug-in and were henceforth used as static artillery.*

Rijeka-Zagreb road, an important Croatian strategic axis, and finally a third offensive from the predominently Serbian region of the Papuk mountains was directed at Pakrac strategic crossroads. Once Pakrac was taken, the Serbs would then push on towards Virovitica on the Hungarian border to cut off western Slavonia from the rest of the country.

Western Slavonia, Croatia's wealthiest province, was already under continuous

# THE JNA UNMASKED

attacks launched from Serbia and Vojvodina.

On 4 October, Serbian generals pulled off a political masterstroke: by resorting to an array of legal technicalities, they seized power, and Belgrade became the head of the Federation.

Thanks to this ploy, the Serbs now controlled the constitutional levers and legalised immediately the mobilisation of the armed forces, unlawfully declared several weeks previously. Since mid-September, reservists were being called up in several regions of Bosnia Herzgovina and, as luck would have it, all of them were Serbs.

The Serbs now controlled all the resources of the military machine as the ranks of the armed forces had already been purged of all hostile and anti-Serbian elements.

Seven months later, another purge took place, and the remaining Tito sympathisers were removed from executive positions.

Feeling that the threat had worsened, Croatian President Franjo Tudjman finally ordered the mobilisation of Croatian forces, but many Croats blamed him for dithering over such an important move.

One third of Croatia was already in Serbian hands and for several months, Tudjman had held back his badly equipped troops from intervening, hoping that the 'Federal Army' would collapse.

Fearing the Serbs' reaction Tudjman husbanded his troops as Croatia waited for international recognition.

But in winter 1991, Croatian towns were burning while Europe looked the other way.

# 1991 SERBIAN WINTER OFFENSIVE

Croatian territories invaded by the Serbian Militia and the JNA

Main fighting zones

Serbian thrusts

## SERBIAN ATTACKS IN CROATIA

*In the autumn of 1991, the Serbian army threw in all its forces to support the militias fighting the newly-created Croatian Republic.*
*Battles raged on several fronts.*
The Dalmatian Front, *opened by the Serbs in September, aimed at creating a corridor linking the Adriatic to the Autonomous Serbian Republic of Krajina.*
The Northern Krajina Front, *where the Croats were successful in August, and captured Glina and Petrinja. However they were checked in front of Sisak and Karlovac.*
The Western Slavonian Front *where, enjoying support from local militias, JNA forces thrust northwards to split Croatia.*
The Eastern Slavonian Front. *One of the wealthiest Croatian provinces, Slavonia became the scene of ferocious fighting. The JNA launched the bulk of its motorised forces there, before turning them on Vukovar.*
The Dubrovnik Front *had little strategic value, but drew its significance from political and cultural reasons, being a famous resort and a source of valuable foreign currency through hordes of tourists.*

51

*Right.*
With assault rifles as their only weapons, Croatian National Guardsmen defended the suburbs of Sisak in September 1991. The advance Serbian elements facing them were equipped with sniping rifles, night vision scopes and bullet-proof vests.

*Below.*
A Croatian T-54 MBT in position near the outskirts of Karlovac, Croatia's second largest city. For months on end this city was heavily shelled by the Serbs and came under fire again in January 1993.

*Far right.*
In September 1991 the Croats set up several light anti-aircaft batteries to protect the Sisak oil refineries from Serbian air strikes. The triple 20mm weapons of the type depicted here proved remarkably efficient against low-flying aircraft.

# THE NORTHE

Of secondary strategic importance, this front brought the Serbs closer to Zagreb and enabled them to threaten two vital Croatian communication and supply lines.

The first was the Zagreb-Belgrade highway, providing a link with eastern Slavonia, and the second, the Rijeka-Zagreb highway, a thoroughfare between Croatia's largest harbour and the capital city of the new state. Supported by the JNA, Serbian militias attacked in August and captured Kostajnica, Blinja, Glina-Vojnik and Slunj as well as the strategic Petrinja crossroads. While a number of Serbs inhabited the region, the Croats made up the bulk of the population. They were forced to leave their villages. The Croatian National Guard vain-

# KRAJINA FRONT

y tried to counter-attack but was no
match for the JNA's tanks and artillery.
Dozens of square miles were lost. At the
end of September, the front settled along
two large natural obstacles - the rivers
Kupa and Sava that merge at Sisak.

The city remained in Croatian hands, and
the front froze solid in the winter of 1992
with combat devolving into static warfare.

With the exception of a Croatian pocket
at Sunja, the Serbs held the southern bank
of the Kupa river. One of their major objectives had been reached when they
severed the Zagreb-Belgrade highway, but
they were checked at Karlovac.

A last attack launched in coordination
with a breakout attempt by the besieged

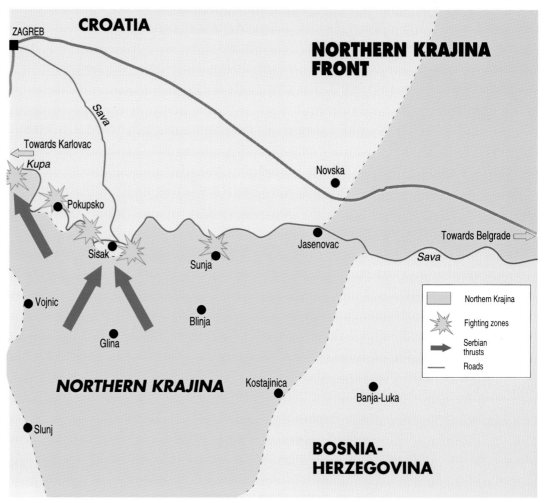

garrison failed in spite of heavy bombing. However, the south-eastern border of 'Greater Serbia' had been outlined.

*In winter 1991, the motley Croatian volunteer units were finally given proper leadership and their officers received adequate training. The Croats began to recapture lost ground as early as December 1991, but this time, they were suitably equipped, as demonstrated by this volunteer clad in an East German padded winter suit.*

*Pictured in December 1991 a few kilometres from Sisak, a Croatian T-54 proceeds to the front line. The recovery of heavy equipment from Federal barracks boosted the morale of the newly-created Croatian army. When the two armies clashed, the difference could soon be seen between reluctant conscripts fighting for ground which wasn't theirs and volunteers defending their homeland.*

*Right.*
A blazing village in the Papuk mountains in western Slavonia. These mountains were easily captured by the Serbs in September 1991, only to be retaken three months later by the newly-created Croatian Army, which suffered severe losses in the process.

*Below.*
The derelict wreck of a Serbian T-54 marks the most advanced Croatian position in the ruins of Novska. During the fighting, all the buildings of this hapless city changed hands several times.

*Below right.*
During the fighting for Novska, the Croats never yielded to their adversaries' overwhelming fire superiority. However, in spite of their grim determination, they only succeeded in retaining half of the city.

# RN SLAVONIAN RONT

Regarded as an objective of only secondary importance, western Slavonia was the scene of some of the fiercest fighting in Croatia. Backed up by Federal forces who had had access to the huge Banja Luka arms depots, the Chetniks infiltrated the mountains, home to important Serbian settlements.

In September, the Papuk mountain range, where Tito intended to stop the Soviets in case of invasion, fell rapidly to the JNA and Serbian militiamen who then swept down on the Croatian villages on the northern side of the range. Their objective was to wrest from the Croats the vital road supplying eastern Slavonia. The Serbs were confident that, once surrounded, this wealthy region would fall into their hands like ripe fruit. But the Croats held their ground and made the most of this difficult terrain where the JNA's heavy equipment lost most of its usefulness. In spite of desperate efforts, the Serbs never captured the cities of Virovitica and Podravska Slatina on the road that skirts the Hungarian border.

In the western end of the pocket, the impor-

*Above.*
*Exhausted Croatian fighters pictured after the seemingly endless combat through the ruins of Pakrac. This city changed hands several times, but finally remained firmly under Croatian control after a fight to the finish.*

*Left.*
*The main street of Novska, opposite the Serbian front lines. The street is lined with wrecked JNA tanks knocked out by the Croats during the bitter fighting that raged there in September and October.*

*Right.*
*His face showing signs of strain, a Croatian soldier is relieved from his position in western Slavonia. This picture is reminiscent of a World War 1 scene, with the trenches, the cold and the mud which characterised that conflict.*

59

tant Pakrac road junction was the scene of bitter fighting and changed hands several times.

Along with Vukovar, Pakrac ranks among the Croatian cities which suffered most from the war.

The Serbs also made unsuccessful attempts to capture Novska, in the western end of the pocket, and Nova Gradiska in the east. But despite incessant bombings and attacks by tanks supported by air force and artillery, the two cities held out soutly and, in December, the Croatian National Guard launched their first counter-

attacks from eastern Slavonia. These counter-attacks were limited but cleverly led in a front where the JNA could never effectively support the Chetniks.

The Papuk range was recaptured and the Serbian militias committed even more atrocities before withdrawing. In Vocin, Croatian policemen were burnt alive and dozens of civilians were slaughtered. In January, only Novska and Nova Gradiska were still threatened by Serbian artillery.

The Serbian salient in western Slavonia had been cleared.

*Left.*
*A further outrage to Tito's defunct Yugoslav Federation: fighters systematically defile, topple or spray with gunfire the statues extolling the virtues of communist heroes, such as the one shown here decked in a gasmask.*

*Right.*
*Heavy fighting involving tanks and artillery raged in the region of Novska, but in spite of their might, the Serbs could not consolidate their gain in western Slavonia. In the picture, a T-54 on strength with the Serbian militia has skidded into a ditch where it provided an excellent anti-tank obstacle for the Croats. Exposed to fire from both sides, it could not be retrieved by either party.*

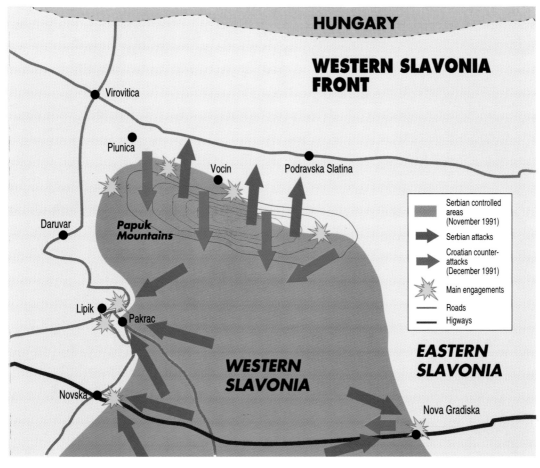

HUNGARY

**WESTERN SLAVONIA FRONT**

Virovitica

Piunica

Vocin

Podravska Slatina

Daruvar

*Papuk Mountains*

Lipik

Pakrac

*WESTERN SLAVONIA*

*EASTERN SLAVONIA*

Novska

Nova Gradiska

Serbian controlled areas (November 1991)

Serbian attacks

Croatian counter-attacks (December 1991)

Main engagements

Roads

Higways

*Right.*
*In the winter of 1991-92,*
*Croatian soldiers scan the*
*the Serbian front lines near*
*Osijek. As the war dragged*
*on, both sides dug in, built*
*bunkers and layed mines to*
*prevent any suprise move by*
*the enemy.*

Closer to Belgrade than Zagreb, this front was of crucial importance to the protagonists. An extension of the large Danubian plain, prosperous eastern Slavonia used to be Yugoslavia's granary, and this region is also purported to hold important oil deposits. Predominantly inhabited by Croats who make up 85% of the population, eastern Slavonia has a few Magyar villages and Serbian settlements amounting to about 10% of the region's denizens. Assisted by the Serbs from the other bank of the Danube, the active Serbian militias were behind the Borovo Selo ambush that sparked off the war.

Only too eager to add this wealthy province to 'Greater Serbia', Belgrade wasted no time in having the JNA give the militias all the sup-

# THE EASTERN SLAVONIAN FRONT

port they needed. Eastern Slavonia's terrain is flat - good tank country - and, on 25 October, an impressive column of 400 tanks and APCs took up position around Sid. At Vukovar, fighting had already been going on for a month and the region north of the River Drava had been captured by Serbian militias. Holding the low ground, the Croats yielded to the Federal forces' crushing superiority but fought tooth and nail for every village.

Despite this desperate resistance, most vil-

lages were lost to the Croats - but at a great cost to the Serbs who suffered frightful losses. Added to internal problems, this bloodbath slowly sapped the morale of the Federal Army. The young conscripts were less and less enthusiastic about the war and increasing numbers of reservists were called in to plug the gaps. Frontal attacks were only entrusted to locally-raised 'Greater Serbian' units supported by Chetniks (such as Major Arkan's men who operated with heavy support from the JNA).

*Above.*
**In the Osijek's Nustar suburbs, HVO soldiers are returning from a patrol. The men are well equipped, as each one is armed with a 7.92mm M-53 machine-gun. Behind them lies the turret of a Serbian M-84 knocked out several weeks before. This MBT was the only tank that broke through Croatian defence lines and penetrated the city before being blasted by anti-tank rockets.**

*Right.*
**Osijek's industrial zone provides the backdrop for this picture, showing a party of Croatian soldiers returning to Osijek after patrolling through no-man's land.**

The Croatian defence revolved around three cities: Vukovar, Vinkovci and Osijek. The latter was one of the Serbs' prime objectives, as they intended to turn it into the capital city of the 'Serbian Republic of Slavonia'.

At the end of September, the Serbs struck at Vukovar with all their might. Outnumbered ten to one, the defenders clung to each house and cellar, and Vukovar soon epitomised resistance to all Croats. But on 17 September, resistance ceased. Out of ammunition, a handful of haggard survivors surrender-ed to the victors. This battle had cost the Federal army 600 armoured vehicles and 50 tanks but worse, the JNA's impetus had been blunted. The only offensive the Federals launched thereafter was at Tenja, south of Osijek. They made no attempt to capture the other besieged cities of Vinkovci and Osijek, limiting their efforts to shelling them instead.

Thanks to the efforts of Vukovar's heroic defenders, the Croats had retained most of their wealthiest province.

**EASTERN SLAVONIA COMBAT ZONES**

HUNGARY

SERBIA

CROATIA

BOSNIA

- Territories captured from the Croats
- Frontline
- Serbian air raids
- JNA and Militia thrusts
- Main engagements
- Roads

Drava · Osijek · Ernestinovo · Laslovo · Borovo · Darovo · Bosut · Nustar · Vukovar · Danube · Vinkovci · Slavonski Brod · Sid · SavA

*Left.*
*Although lack of heavy artillery prevented them from retaliating, the Croats fought back until the 1992 ceasefire by conducting numerous raids and attacks against the Serbian lines. The Croatian flag marks the extreme limit of the friendly-controlled sector.*

*Right.*
*Invisible to Serbian defenders, Croatian commandos launch a surprise attack with mortars, forcing the Serbs to reveal their positions and expose themselves to sniper fire.*

*Below.*
*The marshy approches to Osijek reduced the use of armoured vehicles but also contributed to difficulties in supplying the front lines. This was at its worst during the winter of 1991-92 when Serbian shelling was at its fiercest.*

One of the M-84s destroyed by rockets during the first major offensive launched by the Serbs against Borovo-Naselje, one of Vukovar's suburbs, in September 1991. The vehicle was knocked out when hit in the turret by a 64mm rocket fired from an M-80 rocket launcher. In this engagement involving mostly street fighting, the Serbs lost about 10 M-84 MBTs and M-80 APCs.

# VUKOVAR: CR

# TIA'S STALINGRAD

Above.
*October 1991. Armed wth an M-80 64mm rocket launcher, these Croats are about to fire at a Serbian stronghold they have just spotted. After shooting, they will quickly vanish from the scene to elude the retributory salvoes of mortar shells the Serbs will inevitably fire.*

Few people had heard of Vukovar, a peaceful city nestled in a bend of the Danube, before the Yugoslav conflict hit the headlines. It became famous overnight and its name was mentioned for three months in all the news bulletins. Every day, Radio Belgrade announced that: *'The liberation of Vukovar is close at hand'*.

Outnumbered 10 to one, Vukovar's garrison consisted of a handful of soldiers assisted by 10,000 civilians. This motley force kept the Serbs at bay. Shelled day and night, isolated, without supplies, water and electricity, Vukovar became the symbol of Croatian resistance. Its martyrdom brought home to the world that the 'troubles' in Yugoslavia had degenerated into the first conventional war waged on European soil since 1945

Fighting started on 4 August when the Federal Army launched a major offensive in Slavonia and tried to capture as much ground as possible around Vukovar. In a second move, the Serbs intended to seize the cities of Vinkovci and Osijek. One after the other, the villages fell into the Federal forces' hands and, in less than a month, 80% of eastern Slavonia was under their control. Near the end of August, an armoured battalion reached Borovo-Naselje and broke into its northern suburbs.

This first Federal attack was beaten back with National Guard commandos accounting for the destruction of two MBTs and five APCs. More than 40 Chetniks were killed in this action. But in spite of this success, the situation remained extremely tense. The defenders were a long way from Zagreb and only had a handful of artillery pieces by way of heavy support. The Vinkovci road was soon cut

off, and a makeshift track was improvised across a corn field to bring in supplies. Littered with wrecked cars and decomposing bodies, this vital umbilical cord was the only route through which ammuntion and food could be delivered to embattled Vukovar.

Federal air bases were a short distance away and MiG-21s and Jastrebs dropped their ordnance over the city less than two minutes after takeoff. But the tempo of attacks lessened after two Jastrebs were brought down by SA-7 missiles in September. The defenders counter-attacked with a few T-55s retrieved from ex-Federal barracks, but in a matter of hours, the crushingly superior JNA forces had no difficulty recapturing whatever ground they had lost.

On 17 September, a Federal force of tanks and infantry attacked Borovo. The Croats let the M-84s come close and blasted them at point blank range with anti-tank rockets. To avenge this failure, the Serbs had their artillery and river boats pound the city. Recently arrived from Belgrade, Major Arkan's militiamen wrested the strategically important wheat silos from the Croats and after setting up triple M-55 20mm guns there, swept the streets with enfilading fire. Out of ammunition, the three Croatian 105mm howitzers and obsolete Soviet 76mm pieces could not silence the Serbian guns.

By early in November, Vukovar's situation was desperate. Led by a former JNA officer, Croatian Colonel Dragutin Izai, the total garrison amounted to 1,500 guards, policemen and HOS militiamen. The civilians could no longer leave the cellars whe-

*Above.*
*In October 1991, the defenders of Vukovar realised the hopelessness of their situation and knew that the fall of the city was unavoidable. But their courage only grew accordingly. The closing stages of the fighting were even more terrible, with the Serbs struggling for the capture of every house, cellar and room.*

# THE BATTLE OF VUKOVAR

| | |
|---|---|
| ▨ | Serbian-held zones |
| ▨ | Croatian-held zones |
| — | Frontline (Sept. 1991) |
| — | Frontline (Oct. 1991) |
| 🚜 | Serbian armoured thrusts |
| ⚔ | Serbian artillery |
| 🚢 | Serbian riverboats |
| ✕✕ | Croatian defences |
| ➡ | JNA and Serbian militia thrusts |

Trpinja

Borovo Selo

BOROVO

SERBIA

1

2

VINKOVCI

Nustar

Brsadin

VUKOVAR

1. Bata shoe factory
2. Borovo Naselje Railway Station
3. Federal Barracks

3

Petrovci

Danube

Stari Jankovci

Negoslavci

**CROATIA**

69

re they huddled, and in the hospital exposed to Serbian fire, patients were operated on in the basement. Anaesthetics had run out long ago.

The Croats held out and had to resort to amazing inventiveness and ingenuity to compensate for the inferiority of their weapons. For example, a teenage soldier turned agricultural anti-hail rockets into rifle grenades, and a 12.7mm machine-gun was removed from the hull of a wrecked M-84 and mounted on a trailer. Fitted with makeshift armour plating, the contraption could be seen towed about by an old, battered car riddled like a

*Above.*
*In 1991, the Federal Army was humiliated by the setbacks its suffered at the hands of the Slovenes and yet its officers didn't learn from their mistakes. In October, during the siege of Vukovar, Federal tanks still operated without infantry support in the streets of the beleaguered town and repeatedly took heavy losses. The Serbs took a beating and only won a Pyrrhic victory at Vukovar: they have not tried similar tactics in Croatia since.*

*Left.*
*September 1991. One of the few Croatian artillery pieces in position in the main street of Borovo-Naselje. This 76mm mountain gun accounted for several Serbian armoured vehicles before being knocked out.*

70

sieve. Then there was Julius, head of the local radio ham club, who somehow managed to jam Serbian transmissions.

Later, one of the Montenegrine fighters who had volunteered to 'clean' Croatian strongholds said: *'They're amazingly tenacious. We must fight for every street, every house. Snipers are hiding in every cellar. With their Armbrust rocket launchers, they've knocked down dozens of our tanks and APCs. There are mines and booby traps every-where. It's true hell.'*

18 October marked the beginning of the end. A merciless pounding of the city by M-63 multiple rocket launchers, 105mm, 122mm, and 155mm howitzers signalled the start, then the Serbian troops rushed the Borovo-Naselje railway station. They reached their objective and soon, the two cores of Croatian resistance were split. The next day, from their barracks jutting out into south Vukovar, a column of 250 tanks supported by some 200 infantrymen, broke through the front line and captured part of the southern suburbs. But this didn't keep the Croats from pounding the lost positions with 120mm mortar salvoes. Amazed at their resistance, Veselin Siljivancanin, head of Serbian special units threatened: *'Unless the Croats come out with their hands up, Vukovar will be razed to the ground.'* But in November, the town was still holding out. A light aircraft managed to deliver some supplies, but it was a drop in the ocean. Under a storm of steel and with their ammunition all but exhausted, the 1,500 Croatians held back a mechanised division and two armoured brigades supported by Chetniks, a force of some 20,000 men.

On 17 November, Borovo-Naselje fell. The next day, Croatian commander Mile Dedakovic addressed a radio message to his men and despondently ordered them to lay down their arms. Several hundred Croatian fighters refused to surrender and struggled on for a further 24 hours - to the death. Only a handful fought their way through to Croatian lines.

The siege had lasted 87 days, and the Serbs eventually authorised a Red Cross convoy through to evacuate the civilians. These pictures were seen on television screens around the world and showed a bedraggled mob of elderly people, women and children, filing out of the ruined city. But there were no men among them: they had all died at Vukovar.

*Right.*
*Outnumbered 10 to one, the Croatian defenders of Vukovar held out for 87 days and kept the Serbs out of Slavonia. When fighting was over, the survivors were shot by the Serbs in the ruins of the battered town.*

This terrible but unavoidable setback gave the Croats an additional three months to bolster their defence. President Tudjman later came under fire for not reinforcing the town, but did he really have the choice? The fall of Vukovar would have led to the loss of badly needed heavy equipment that was in critically short supply. The valiant defenders of Vukovar had immobilised the cream of the Federal forces during three crucial months. Vukovar's resistance also had an incredible morale boosting effect and welded the Croats together against the Serbs. Patriotic songs were written about Vukovar, and the heroic resistance of the city was even celebrated on television. One month later, bills were posted on Osijek's walls proclaiming, *'If Vukovar made it, why not us?'*

Vukovar's resistance contributed to Croatia being recognised as an independent state: to the world at large, the Serb had clearly become the aggressor while Croatia had showed that a nation with such an indomitable spirit had earned the right to independence. The Serbs had won a Pyrrhic victory and were weakened by their success. They acknowledged the loss of about 50 tanks, 200 armoured vehicles, and certainly played down or hid other losses from their home public opinion.

Vukovar had blunted the cutting edge of the Serbian armed forces and this marked the beginning of the end for the JNA.

During the siege, Vukovar's garrison never amounted to more than 1,500 soldiers, and it is to these gallant men that Croatia owes its independence.

# ANTI-TANK WEAPONS

Around Vukovar, as on most Croatian battle-fields, light anti-tank weapons played a major role and often provided the only defence against the Serbian onslaught.

Needless to say, it takes nerves of steel and exceptional courage to blast a tank at close range - but there was never any shortage of pluck on either side.

At Osijek, a foreign volunteer told us: *'It is well nigh impossible to destroy a tank from the front, where its armour is at its thickest and its armament can cover a very wide area. To destroy a tank, the anti-tank teams operated in three groups: one was tasked with diverting the attention of the crew while the two others approached the tank from behind and fired into the thinly armoured engine bay bet-*

*Above right.*
*A member of the Croatian armed forces in position with his German-made Armbrust rocket launcher. This weapon proved invaluable for street fighting in Slovenia, Croatia and Bosnia Herzegovina. When the war broke out, the Croats had plentiful quantities of Armbrusts, and had it not been for these rocket launchers, they would have been powerless against the Serbian onslaught.*

*Right.*
*Pictured in Vukovar, this Croatian volunteer presents the most widely used rocket launcher on issue to both sides: the RBR M-80. This 64mm disposable weapon can only knock out lightly armoured and soft-skinned vehicles. The Serbs also use the RBR M-80 against buildings and as bunker busters.*

ween the exhaust pipes. Only the rear of the tank is vulnerable to light rocket launchers. But it's a dangerous game, and inevitably, we always lost one or two men in such attacks.' Croatian fighters made heavy use of Armbrusts and RPG-7s, and also employed the excellent anti-tanks weapons on issue to the JNA.

The anti-tank inventory includes:

The wire-guided AT-7 Sagger, known as 'Maliutka' by the soldiers of both sides who fire it from the ground or from the turrets of BOV and M-80 combat vehicles. With a 2,500m range, this weapon has proved extremely efficient on the Slavonian plains and in the Bosnian valleys.

The Federal forces also use more modern AT-4 Spigot missiles, and 82mm recoilless guns. This wheeled gun fires a shell capable of piercing 220mm of armour plating from 1,000m. Easily and quickly set up, this gun must be rapidly moved after each shot, as its position will inevitably be given away by the cloud of smoke emitted by its ammunition.

### The M-57 rocket launcher

Yugoslav-built version of the World War 2 German Panzerfaust. The 144mm tube launches a rocket capable of piercing 300mm of armour plating from 200m.

### The M-79 rocket launcher

On standard issue to the Yugoslav army, the M-79 is identical to the French LRAC and has the same 90mm calibre. Weighing 6.2kg, the M-79 fires a 3.5kg rocket over a 600m range. Its hollow-charge warhead will penetrates 400mm of armour plating.

### The RBR M-80 rocket launcher

Used profusely by fighters on both side, this light

rocket launcher is the Yugolsav version of the US M-72 LAW. Very efficient against lightly armoured or soft-skinned vehicles, this one-shot, disposable rocket launcher is also intensively used for urban fighting. With a 64mm calibre, the M-80 can penetrate 400mm of armour plating from 250m.

### The Armbrust

Designed for minimal smoke, flash and noise, this discreet German-made rocket launcher proved highly efficient in street fighting. Relatively small, the Armbrust is 850mm long and weighs 6.3kg. Its round can pierce 300mm of armour plating.

*Above.*
*In Bosnia, this Muslim volunteer is setting up an AT-7 Sagger anti-tank missile. This wire-guided missile can also be fired from a vehicle or a tank turret.*

Located on the northern plains of eastern Slavonia, Osijek is the capital city of this province that stretches some 350km east from Zagreb. Overlooking the Drava river, Osijek was subjected to heavy bombing during winter 1991. However, the spirited defence of Vukovar checked the Serbian onslaught and gave the Croats the respite they needed to bring in reinforcements. This dissuaded the Serbs from launching a costly attack.

It all started at the end of summer and, as everywhere else in Croatia, the events unfolded according to the now well-known pattern: supported by regular forces, Serbian militias infiltrated the area and had soon gained control of the whole region north of the Drava. Only a thin strip of land remained under Croatian control when, in October, the Federal Army intervened with heavy elements. After fierce fighting, the villages of Ernestinovo and Laslovo were captured. In the latter, Croatian guardsmen destroyed six tanks before being forced out. Osijek was now besieged and only the Valpovo road

*Above.*
**Unlike the inhabitants of Vukovar who were evacuated, the population of Osijek took an active part in the defence of the city when fighting raged on the outskirts during the bitter months of the winter 1991-1992. Young women posted bills extolling the virtues of Croatian fighters.**

running to the west along the Hungarian border kept the city supplied with arms and ammunition.

*'Osijek will hold out and will not be another Vukovar'*, screamed the posters on the city's walls.

While the majority of the population had been evacuated, numerous inhabitants felt they had to stay put to contribute to their city's defence by assisting the soldiers.

After licking the wounds received at Vukovar,

# OSIJEK

*Left.*
*In January 1992, Croatian commandos leap out of a ditch before crossing into no-man's land to explore a building. The Serbian lines were less than 100m away.*

*Below.*
*In position near Osijek, one of the M-36B2 tank destroyers recovered by the Croats and on strength with their forces. Although obsolete, these World War 2 vintage vehicles played a significant part in the defence of the town.*

# DER SIEGE

the Federal Army launched a formidable offensive on Tenja, the last Croatian stronghold to the south of the city. Preceded by a deluge of fire from artillery and multiple rocket launchers, 30 M-84s thundered into the main street of the village. The Croatian National Guard was slowly forced back. A forlorn machine-gun position held out for two hours, but at dawn on 5 December, it was all over. The last Croatian outpost had fallen.

The Serbian tanks could fire over open sights at Osijek's outer suburbs. But this time, the garrison was ready and waiting for them. Energetically led by Major Glavash, the defence had been organised into three lines reinforced with minefields and anti-tank obstacles. The defenders had little heavy armament - a few M-36 tank destroyers, T-55s, and a battery of 155mm howitzers. There were about 15,000 soldiers in Osijek waiting for the Serbs, and the garrison included battle-hardened veterans.

The assailants contented themselves with shelling the city. Both sides dug in, but the garrison of Osijek didn't stay inactive and the platoon of foreign volunteers, led by a Catalonian, kept the Serbs on their toes by raiding their lines. Known as the Obuka Commando, this unit was composed mostly of former Foreign Legion personnel.

Several night raids were conducted by a large Antonov An-2 crop duster converted into a bomber, and this aircraft dropped makeshift bombs over the Serbian headquarters in Ten-

*Above.*
*In the winter of 1991-92, Croatian fighters, despite being under fire, bring in an ammunition crate to the foremost defence line in Osijek. Unlike Croatian cities that were often captured without a fight, the Slavonian towns always held their own and never capitulated to the vastly superior Serbian units.*

*Far right.*
*February 1992. A modified M-60PB on strength with Croatian forces heads for its combat position in the suburbs of Osijek. The vehicle mounts an 82mm recoilless gun.*

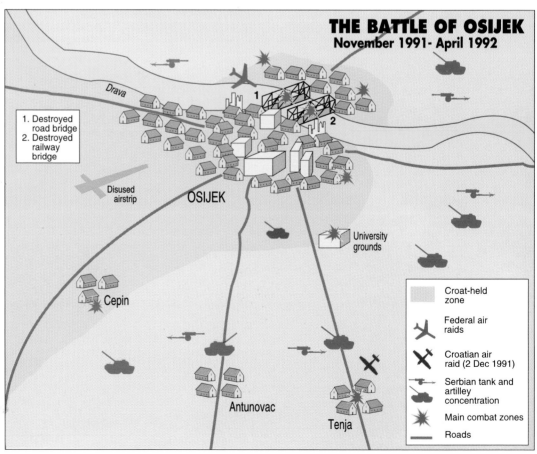

**THE BATTLE OF OSIJEK**
**November 1991 - April 1992**

1. Destroyed road bridge
2. Destroyed railway bridge

Drava

Disused airstrip

OSIJEK

University grounds

Cepin

Antunovac

Tenja

Croat-held zone

Federal air raids

Croatian air raid (2 Dec 1991)

Serbian tank and artilley concentration

Main combat zones

Roads

ja, killing one militia leader. Almost every night, Serbian artillery pounded the city, initially concentrating its fire on the inner area prior to shelling the outer suburbs and front line positions.

But the major assault never came and the few desultory Serbian attacks were easily repelled. A crisis of morale was already sweeping through the Federal ranks and  dissension between officers only made things worse for the Serbian forces. Croatian determination had withstood the might of the Serbs who had found that crushing armour superiority was of no avail in urban fighting. They also knew that they would have to wrest Osijek from the Croats house by house. Scalded by its Vukovar experience, the JNA gave up. Osijek marked a turning point in the war: the Serbian war machine had stalled badly in Croatia.

In January, a ceasefire was signed and UN troops were expected. But in April 1992, seven civilians were killed by shelling ordered by the Serbs in retaliation for a Croatian raid on their own lines.

*Right.*
*Vukovar fell in November 1991, but thanks to the spirited leadership of its mayor, the city of Osijek was spared the fate of its martyred neighbour by providing itself with anti-tank defences and bunkers. Although Zagreb's government denied the Vukovar defenders the heavy armament they requested, it did not hesitate to bolster the defence of Osijek by providing the garrison with weapons like this Model 43 120mm mortar.*

*Right.*
*As the plains of eastern Slavonia are devoid of natural obstacles, the Croats had to resort to much ingenuity and courage to stem the edvance of Serbian armoured columns after the fall of Vukovar in November 1991.*

# THE NEXT TARGET: VINKOVCI

*Far right.*
*Members of Croatia's 1st Special Forces Battalion shelling Serbian front lines with mortars during a surprise attack in January 1992. After firing several salvoes, the Croats quickly withdrew to safer positions before the Serbs had time to recover and retaliate.*

On 17 November 1991, the garrison of Vukovar laid down its arms after a heroic but hopeless struggle and the town of Vinkovci, farther south, was the JNA's next target.

To the west of the city, Federal tanks were a few hundred metres away from its outlying suburbs.

To the north east, on the road to Vukovar, the small village of Nustar was besieged on three sides and under repeated attacks. But this Croatian outpost held out.

Only on one occasion did a Serbian M-84 MBT break through the front line and into the village, but it was soon knocked out in the main street. During the 1991-92 winter, Nustar and Vinkovci expected major attacks but they never materialised. The Serbs made the most of their heavy artillery and contented themselves with shelling the town with impunity.

The Croatians were not idle and HOS teams often sneaked out and raided Serbian lines. In April 1992, Russian Blue Helmets were deployed in the area while the Serbs reinforced their grip on the territories they occupied by building a defensive line strengthened with concrete bunkers.

The Croats knew that they had to recapture Vukovar, and that a hard task lay ahead.

*A party of foreign volunteers fighting on the Croatian side pictured during the winter of 1991-92. For months, volunteers defended Osijek while this Slavonian city was subjected to a remorseless siege. The bulk of foreign volunteers came from Europe principally from France, Britain, Spain and Germany. Their ranks also included a few Americans and Australians. Always engaged in the thickest of the fighting, they suffered heavy losses.*

# FOREIGN VOLUN

Foreigners began to join the Croatian ranks as soon as the situation became serious in 1991. When hostilities escalated, increasing numbers of foreigners joined the ranks of the Croatian National Guard. However, there were two different groups of foreigners - foreign-born Croats who, for the most part, hailed from the United States, Canada, Argentina and Australia, and who had left their country of birth to defend what they regard as their proper homeland.

The other group was that of genuine foreign volunteers who originated mostly from Britain, France and Germany, and who took sides

# 'ERS IN CROATIA

with Croatia for various reasons, ranging from sheer idealism to a craving for adventure. These men fought bravely and their military expertise benefited the Croats (many British volunteers were ex-Foreign Legion).

With the exception of a small, Osijek-based elite unit led by Catalonian Captain Eduardo Flors, no Croatian unit was exclusively composed of foreigners, and most of them were scattered individually or in small groups among regular Croatian Guard forces.

With their monthly wages amounting to about £3, greed can hardly be regarded as their prime motivation.

*In the spring of 1992, Dubrovnik's Croatian outposts were equipped with artillery batteries and could fire back at Serbian forces. In the picture, Croats have set up a Soviet M-42 57mm gun.*

# THE DALMATIAI

Stretching over 800km, this front was a nightmare for the Croatian forces. Too narrow to be adequately strengthened, it was thinly defended because the only heavy weapons the Croatian National Guard possessed had been allocated to the defence of Zagreb.

The Serbian war aims in Dalmatia were now clear:
- To give 'Greater Serbia' the maritime outlet it had always sought. This would be achieved by military conquest followed by ethnic cleansing.
- Control the coastal road linking Rijeka, Zadar, Split and Dubrovnik to prevent supplies from reaching the Dalmatian coast.
- Conquer Herzegovina, the part of the Bosnian Republic predominently inhabited by Serbs.

On this front more than on any other, bridges had a crucial importance. Only large road and railway bridges link the mainland to the Dalmatian islands, and enable the coastal road to

*Above.*
*A Croatian T-34/85 MBT defending the approaches of Dubrovnik from Serbian-Montenegrine forces. The threat to this region was removed when the suburbs of Trebinje, in the north of Dubrovnik, were captured by the Croatian army in the autumn of 1992. The extra anti-missile protection on the vehicle's hull and turret is noteworthy.*

cross over bays and sounds.

In September 1991, Serbian militias and JNA armoured support rushed in from the Knin region and headed northwest for the coast. The assailants reached the Adriatic Sea to the south of Karlobag, captured the strategic bridge at Maslenica (but couldn't prevent its destruction) before being checked in front of Gospic. The Zadar and Sibenik bridges were saved in the nick of time by a handful of Croats who also stopped an armoured column a few kilometres away from the vital Sibenik bridge in the suburbs of Zadar.

By the end of September, the Serbs had nearly achieved all their objectives, and the coastal road had been cut off. A month later, the front had stabilised. The Croats made several unsuc-

# FRONT

*A Croatian tank crew on the front line in the northern region of Split. Although underequipped and short on heavy armament when fighting broke out in August 1991, the volunteers of the Croatian brigades stemmed the Serbian armoured onslaught.*

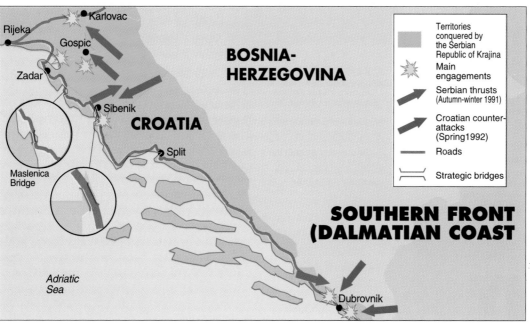

Rijeka

Karlovac

Gospic

Zadar

**BOSNIA-HERZEGOVINA**

Sibenik

**CROATIA**

Split

Maslenica Bridge

*Adriatic Sea*

Dubrovnik

**SOUTHERN FRONT (DALMATIAN COAST**

Territories conquered by the Serbian Republic of Krajina

Main engagements

Serbian thrusts (Autumn-winter 1991)

Croatian counter-attacks (Spring 1992)

Roads

Strategic bridges

*Above right.*
*Zagreb's soldiers deployed on the Dalmatian coast and in southern Croatia had to make use of all kinds of craft and boats to keep Dubrovnik supplied. The Croats also fought the Serbian navy in engagements involving grossly disproportionate forces.*

*Right.*
*A T-55 on strength with the Tiger Brigade, one of Zagreb's elite units, pictured near the town of Zadar. One of the Serbs' major objectives in the autumn of 1991, Zadar was never captured. Issued with the best equipment the Croatian Army could offer, the Tigers were used as a fire brigade unit all over Croatia.*

cessful attempts to recapture the Maslenica bridge. Totally outgunned, the National Guard gave in to the Serbs who were shelling Zadar, and who occupied the airport and almost everything short of capturing the harbour. The Federal Air Force attempted to destroy the Miletici and Sibenik bridges, but only succeeded in causing heavy damage to both. The destruction of the Maslenica bridge was a hard blow for the Serbs and they had to resort to ferries and barges to get between the Dalmatian coast and island of Pag.

In October, the Serbs used the attacks on the Federal barracks as a pretext to encircle and besiege the historical city of Dubrovnik. Predominently Croatian, this city had a large tourist and cultural interest but hardly any strategic value. Swollen by the mass of refugees sweeping in from the country, the population lived stoically through bombings and shelling by air, sea and land. Although the extent of the damage to historical buildings has been exaggerated, the modern part of the city has suffered extensively from the bombings. In April 1992, the first Blue Helmets were deployed on the Zadar front, but the UN forces' control did not extend to Dubrovnik and to the southern front. Meanwhile, the Croats launched one of their first counter-attacks to recapture lost ground around Dubrovnik.

In May and June, the National Guard assisted by 1st Brigade (nicknamed the Tiger Brigade) launched local attacks along the coast in the direction of Dubrovnik. At first, the Serbs put up a spirited defence but broke and collapsed near the village of Slano. This success opened the way to Dubrovnik which was finally relieved. Croatian losses amounted to about 50 men. Dubrovnik was now out of the range of Serbian 81mm mortars but was still exposed to heavy artillery fire. The front stabilised in June, with the Croatian troops poised on the approaches to Montenegro and within reach of the guns of the large Kotor Naval Base, the new homeport of the Federal Navy since it had lost use of the Croatian harbours.

The Croats had another military success when they stormed the Drnis plateau on 21 June, but this was followed by a diplomatic setback. Abandoned in the previous September by its inhabitants, the Croats intended to relocate some 20,000 refugees in the city of Drnis. Taking advantage of the slackness of the Kenyan Blue Helmets who were controlling the site, 200 Croatian commandos crossed the river in kayaks and infiltrated the Serbian positions. At dawn, they launched a two-pronged attack aimed at the front and flank of the Serbian positions. Taken aback, the Serbian militias asked for reinforcements, but their counter-attack failed disastrously and the plateau remained in Croatian hands. Diplomatic pressure however, later forced the Croats to abandon their prized capture.

# THE BLUE HELME

*Above.*
**A VAB on strength with 1er RIMa 'Marsouins' on duty on the front line in the Croatian town of Karlovac. This area suffered extensive damage in the fighting of winter 1991-92. Karlovac was again exposed to Serbian artillery fire when the Croats thrust towards the Dalmatian coast in January 1993.**

*Right.*
**For months on end, French Blue Helmets patrolled along the roads of the demilitarised zone officially known as 'pink zones'. Shown here is a VBL from 2e RIMa, armed with a 7.62mm machine-gun, and pictured in the Velebit Mountains which run along Croatia's eastern coast.**

ARRIVE

*Above.*
*On 31 March 1992, the French Blue Helmets boarded a car ferry and the TCD Orage assault ship, and were shipped to Rijeka, Croatia.*
*p 89*

*Above right.*
*Various supply vehicles on strength with the logistics battalion before embarking at Toulon. This unit was headquartered in Zagreb during its assignment in Croatia. France contributed the largest number of troops to the UNPROFOR deployment.*

*Above right.*
*Crammed to overflowing, TCD Orage berthing in Toulon. On the rear deck can be seen Berliet GBC trucks. These ubiquitous vehicles are currently used by the French Blue Helmets deployed in the Balkans and in Cambodia.*

On 21 February 1992, the United Nations Security Council approved Resolution 743 allowing the intervention of an international force in what used to be Yugoslavia. Known as UNPROFOR, this force was initially scheduled to be deployed for 12 months. In agreement with the protagonists, UNPROFOR had to implement the famous 'Vance-Owen Plan', the main points of which were:
- creating a buffer between the Serbs and the Croats.
- disarming the militias.
- supervising the departure of the 'Federal' Army.
- restoring the communication network.
- allowing the return home of the refugees.
According to the plan, Croatia (and the territories annexed by the Serbs) would be subdivided into northern, western, southern and eastern zones, and would be occupied by infantry battalions provided by 12 countries. France would contribute the heaviest complement of troops.

In April, the first Blue Helmets took up their allocated positions. Fighting didn't stop imme-

diately but gradually abated. However, Osijek was shelled for well over a month after the arrival of Belgian and Russian Blue Helmets, and the Kenyan Battalion was powerless when the Croats attacked Drnis on 21 June 1992.

The UN forces deployed successfully but soon suffered their first losses. In June, a Belgian stepped on a landmine in Baranja, and two French officers were killed by a remote-controlled charge at Zadar Airport on 17 July 1992. However, it became obvious that the UN forces lacked teeth when the Blue Helmets proved incapable of disarming the Serbs, and had to content themselves with placing the militias' heavy equipment in UN-controlled depots.

The Blue Helmets also failed to repatriate the refugees expelled from the Serbian-held areas.

*Following pages.*
*Pictured near Osijek, eastern Slavonia in September 1992, a Belgian member of 1er Cycliste enforcing the cease-fire from the turret of his IFV. The vehicle is armed with a 12.7mm heavy machine-gun.*

89

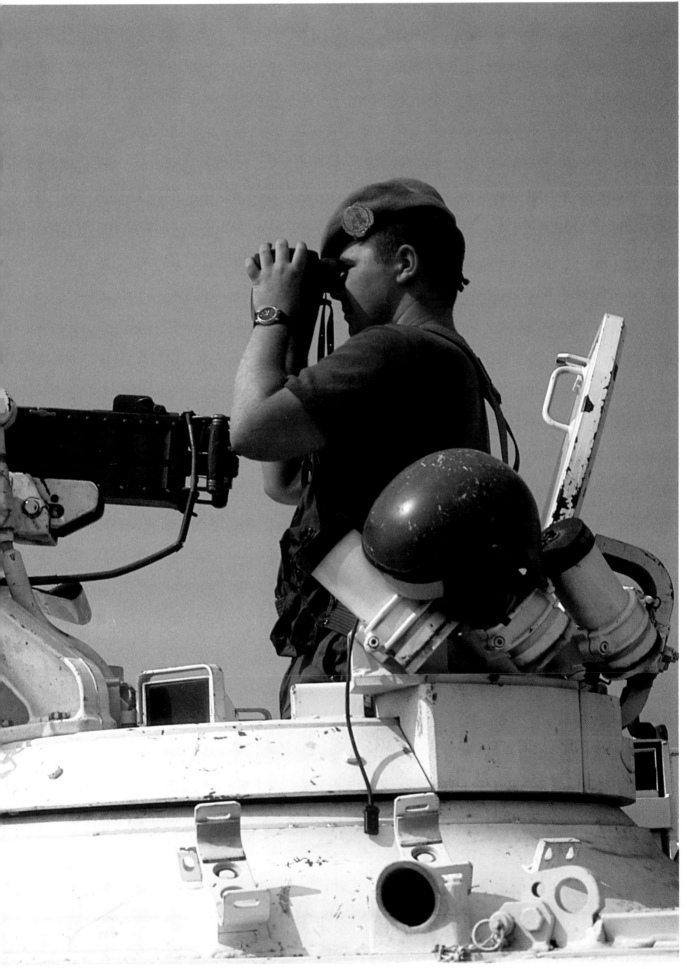

*Above.*
**With his blue helmet on, this Russian para is on duty at a checkpoint in eastern Slavonia. This was Russia's first participation in a UN mission, and it contributed some 900 men to the first UNPROFOR deployment.**

*Above right.*
**Jordanian Blue Helmets controlling vehicles on the Zagreb-Belgrade highway. Traffic on this road has been scant since it was cut off in the spring of 1991, and only portions are now open to the few cars that dare to venture there. The Jordanian Infantry Battalion was based at Novska, western Slavonia.**

*Right.*
**In the heartland of Krajina, Blue Helmets of 4th Coy, 2e RIMa exchange orders after returning from a patrol. Deployed in a sensitive zone, some French units were caught in the crossfire when the Croats launched their major attack in January 1993.**

*Above right.*
*A Russian Blue Helmet conducts routine checks before a UN convoy crosses the dangerous zone between the Croatian and Serbian lines in the Tenja area, near Osijek. In spite of a cease-fire agreement signed in February 1992, peace never prevailed here,with armed clashes following bombings*

*Right.*
*Two Czech Blue Helmets pictured on 2 September 1992 in front of a BRDM-2 armoured vehicle. These men were on duty at one of the checkpoints set up around the city of Titova Korenica on the Bosnian-Croatian border south of Bihac. Although their means were limited, these soldiers performed satisfactorily, and never gave in under pressure.*

*Above.*
*At the end of December 1992, the French Blue Helmets were relieved by elements provided by France's 3rd Army Corps. The initial deployment consisted of 'Marsouins' from RIMa and RICM. French units were among those that were the most heavily committed in Croatia, impounding most of the protagonists' heavy weapons, clearing vast quantities of mines and ordnance, and escorting humanitarian convoys to Bihac, a Muslim enclave besieged by the Serbs in Bosnia.*

*Right.*
*In the autumn of 1992, Belgian Blue Helmets are seen manning a checkpoint in eastern Slavonia. The Belgians soon had to handle most of the assignments in this sector after the Russians who supported them had all but given up. The Belgians went about their task diligently and executed their orders strictly, unlike the badly paid and poorly motivated Russians who often sympathised with the Serbs.*

*Right.*
Near Bosanski Brod, a newly-enlisted Croatian volunteer watches as his house burns during the advance of Serbian armoured columns at the end of April 1992.

*Below.*
**May 1992. Serbian militias have just been chased out of Kolibe, 15km south of Bosanski Brod, after slaughtering about 30 Muslims and Croatian civilians. Recaptured by Croatian and Muslim forces, the village fell into Serbian hands again after a massive attack supported by tanks and artillery.**

# WAR
# BOSNIA

*Below.*
*November 1992. In north-western Bosnia, not far from the Bihac pocket, a member of Croatia's 128th Brigade is about to fire a salvo of Model 60 rifle grenades from a makeshift launcher. The Bihac railway junction was one of the Serbs' main objectives as it played a vital role in keeping Krajina supplied.*

# READS TO
# RZEGOVINA

*Right.*
*Spring 1992. A brand new T-55 on strength with the Croatian forces pictured on the western Herzegovinan front. To assist their fellows in that republic, the Croatian army crossed the border with 30 MBTs to check the Serbs who were trying trying to cut the communication lines and capture as much ground as possible.*

## CROATIA

- Zenica
- Bugojno
- Sibenik
- Jasce
- Kupres
- Split

## SOUTHERN FRONT (BOSNIA-HERZEGOVINA)

- SARAJEVO

## BOSNIA-HERZEGOVINA

- Mostar
- Goradze
- Trebinje
- Dubrovnik

Serbian-controlled zones

Croation-controlled zones

Muslim-controlled zones

Main engagements

Serbian thrusts

Croatian thrusts

Road

*Adriatic Sea*

*Above.*
**Pictured in the Bihac pocket during the autumn of 1992, a Bosnian fighter observes the Serbian front line. The pocket was totally encircled and in some places, the front lines were only a few hundred metres apart. For months, the poorly armed Bosnian territorial forces were exposed to Serbian shelling and couldn't retaliate for want of artillery.**

The symbol of a multi-ethnic republic as envisaged by Tito, Bosnia Herzegovina proclaimed its independence in October 1991, and managed to keep out of the conflict until February 1992 when bloody clashes between Serbs and Croats flared up in the Mostar region, a predominently Serbian area. On Saturday, 29 February, more than four million Bosnians went to the polling booths when the question of independence was subjected to a ballot, and 99.4% of those who voted declared themselves in favour of autonomy (turnout was 66%).

In early March, the Bosnian Serbs were staunchly determined to check the process of independence and erected roadblocks in the streets of Sarajevo. The large avenue to the airport as well as all the roads leading out of the city were blocked off. The Serbs refused to become a minority in a Muslim-controlled state and took up arms. The attitudes which had led to the war

in Croatia were repeating themselves in Bosnia.

In less than 30 days, barricades were up on all the roads into Serbian, Croatian and Muslim villages. The country, especially Sarajevo, geared up for war. The militias took control of the capital city and the first snipers made their appearance. UN soldiers who had no mandate to intervene in Bosnia would have to tackle another conflict.

In the early days of May, the headquarters of the UN forces left Sarajevo. This was followed by fighting, sporadic at first, but soon degenerating into full scale engagements. In Herzegovina, Serbian forces and Croatian units were fighting it out with heavy weapons.

In less than two weeks, the young republic was ablaze. Soon, the war would become more terrible there — possibly worse — than in neighbouring Croatia.

*Above right.*
*Armed with a Mauser rifle fitted with a scope, a Croatian soldier fires at the Serbian outposts on the opposite bank of the Sava river in northern Bosnia. Month after month, the Serbs suffered high losses in their relentless attacks to consolidate their position - and also massacred the Muslim and Croatian population.*

*Right.*
*At the end of 1992, a Croatian unit is about to set off for the front line near Derventa in northern Bosnia. Lack of suitable leadership led to the Croats losing that town to the Serbs who also captured the important road junction that helped keep Croatian Krajina supplied.*

*Right.*
*Firing from a Muslim cemetery, Armija fighters flush out Serbian snipers concealed in a forest near Bugojno, Herzegovina. In the spring of 1992, this region was the scene of ferocious fighting between Serbian and Croatian forces.*

**ARMY**

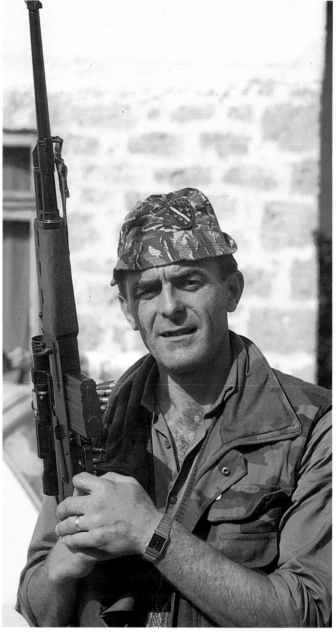

Descended from the Territorial Forces of Bosnia Herzegovina, the Bosnian Army (or Armija) had a theoretical establishment of 150,000 men when it was called up in the winter of 1992-93. But Armija's real strength was closer to 45,000 soldiers.

A heterogenous conglomerate, Armija's ranks included Muslims, Croats and Serbs mustered in units of varying sizes.

Often, each unit only defended its own village and fields. Sorely underequipped, the Bosnians displayed great courage when they captured heavy weapons stores from the Federal barracks in spring 1992.

The forces became more unbalanced in the winter of 1992 when the Bosnians turned against their erstwhile Croatian allies and lost several key positions in central Bosnia.

By the winter of 1993, the Bosnians fielded about 15 T-54 and T-55 MBTs, some 20 artillery pieces, 100 recoilless guns and 200 mortars to oppose the might of Serbia's 350 MBTs and 1,000 artillery pieces.

Armija was always critically short of heavy weapons and its effort to increase its armament was hampered by the Croats who enforced the UN embargo by impounding all the equipment the Bosnians purchased abroad and shipped through their territory.

Whether in Sarajevo or in eastern Bosnia, all Bosnian attacks failed in spite of the unflinching courage displayed by Armija fighters.

*Above left and above.*
*In the spring of 1992, the whole population of Bosnia Herzegovina was called up for service with the territorial defence forces. Most were Muslims, but the ranks of the territorial forces also included many Serbs and Croats. People from all walks of life took up arms and fought under the lily emblem. Underequipped, but not short on courage, these fighters were massacred when they came up against the Serbs in Bosnia.*

*Above right and far right.*
*Bosnian volunteers in the Bihac pocket, and in eastern Herzegovina.*

*Right.*
*Autumn 1992: handing out assignments before an operation near Bihac.*

In the early months of the war, the poorly organised and under-equipped Armija lost huge tracts of Bosnia Herzegovina, and abandoned countless cities and villages to Serbian militias and regular units.

Officially created on 14 May 1992, the armed forces of the new republic were organised into seven commands and 75 local defence zones. But Armija could not stem the major offensives the Serbs launched in mid-July to capture the strategic cities and crossroads at Bugojno, at Kupres, Mostar, Gorazde (besieged for several months), Knjic, and Odzak.

During the the autumn of 1992, the Serbs conquered 70% of Bosnia's territory and, but for a few Muslim enclaves, hardly anything stood in their way. In the west, the Muslims grimly hung on to the now famous Bihac area, described in April 1992 as 'the bone across Serbia's throat, a zone stretching over 60km for a depth of 50, and inhabited by about 400,000 persons (90% of them are Muslims).

Defence was provided by some 5,000 front-line fighters, organised into the six brigades composing Bosnia's 5th Corps, and backed up by one single T-54. Weapons were either captured or purchased from Krajina's Serbian militiamen who preferred to sell them rather than having them kept under lock and key by UN peacekeepers. A makeshift air strip was built

to complement the supplies trickling into the enclave. Humanitarian help was exclusively provided by the Blue Helmets of the French Battalion, whose magnificent efforts were often underestimated by the Bosnians. The front lines were only four kilometres away from Bihac, and the city was long exposed to fire from enemy 155mm guns and 120mm mortars.

In the south east of Bosnia, the Goradze enclave had been besieged since 4 May. From their positions overlooking the city, the Serbs launched attack after attack but never succeeded in clearing the salient. Casualties among the 100,000 inhabitants and refugees were heavy and soon amounted to 2,000 killed. Shelled for months on end, the population was deprived of supplies and cut off from the outside world. As for the defenders, they had no heavy weapons.

# POCKETS OF BO

Bosnian military command

Bosnian regions held by the Croats and the Muslims (February 1992)

Muslim pockets encircled by units of the Serbian Republic of Bosnia

Serbian attacks

**BOSNIAN RESISTANCE POCKETS**

But somehow, the Bosnians organised their defence forces into two brigades and eventually relieved the pressure by defeating the Serbs who were rolled back over several kilometres, leaving behind their dead, wounded, armament and materiel.

In order to be in a better bargaining situation in case negotiations were initiated, the Serbs set their sights on new territories and attacked again in the winter of 1992-93. To everybody's suprise, they captured the strategic town of Jajce in central Bosnia.

A chill wind of panic swept through the Bosnians who were still defending several cities from the Croats. In mid-February, the Serbs struck massively to stamp out the Srebrenica enclave and capture the Muslim territories along the Drina.

There again, every village in this strategically important region was razed, and the inhabitants expelled or killed. From Cerska, 5,000 people were already fleeing on foot across the Majevica mountains and heading for the Bosnian town of Tuzla.

The heroic defence of this Muslim salient passed unnoticed and, like many other desperate actions, was largely ignored in the west.

# IAN RESISTANCE

*Main pic*
*Members of the Obuka Comma*
*one of Croatia's special u*
*sweeping through a town in south*
*Herzegovina. In the spring of 1.*
*HVO forces recaptured territories f*
*the Serbs who had outrun their su*
*lines in the Serbian-dominated re*
*of Bosnia. The foremost soldi*
*armed with a Model 53 7.92*
*machine-*

*Top.*
*Often well equipped, Croatian units in Bosnia Herzegovina have more than held their own against the Serbs ever since fighting broke out in this republic. The picture shows a Croatian sniper equipped with a folding butt 7.62mm FAL with scope.*

*Left.*
*In spring 1992, the Croats wrested back Mostar from the Serbs, but the city suffered heavily in the process. The bridges were destroyed and large parts of the city were laid waste. The defenders of the Serbian quarter fought to the last man. To support their brethren in Bosnia Herzegovina and stem the Serbian thrusts, Zagreb covertly sent combat units equipped with heavy weapons.*

# THE CROATIAN ARMED FORCES

In spring 1992, the Croatian government in Zagreb realised that war was imminent in Bosnia Herzegovina, and discreetly dispatched there several brigades from the newly created Croatian Army.

Their mission was to defend their Croatian brethren, and they found themselves pitted against the ex-Federal Army in strategic sectors such as Kupres, Mostar and Trebinje.

When the Bosnian Republic disintegrated, the Croatian armed forces were recreated as HVO (Hrvatska Voiska Obrambene) and soon fielded several brigades totalling 35,000 men.

Thanks to Zagreb's assistance, most of these brigades were adequately equipped but suffered from poor leadership and lack of heavy weapons. Only the capture in the summer of ex-JNA stores enabled the Croats to acquire about 100 MBTs, 30 APCs, 100 artillery pieces and more than 300 mortars.

With this extra equipment, the Croats established a defence line which checked the Serbs, and later counter-attacked at Bugojno, Mostar and Gradacac.

In October, the Croats managed to cut off for several hours the vital Serbian supply corridor at Brcko in northern Bosnia.

During the winter of 1992-93, the Croatian forces in Bosnia Herzegovina consolidated their positions and supported the right flank of the army attacking Zadar on the Dalmatian coast, in January 1993.

*Above.*
*Entrenched at Kiseljak, north west of Sarajevo, several Croatian heavy units often used field and anti-aircraft guns in the direct support role, as shown here by this quadruple piece composed of 12.7mm heavy machine-guns taken from an aircraft.*

*Right.*
*Croatian soldiers observing the Serbian lines from their positions by the Livno road. Their enemies are only a few hundred metres away. In the spring of 1992, the Serbians thrust from Krajina to sever communication lines in Bosnia-Herzegovina, but their offensive was checked by the Croatian Army. The Serbs lost several tanks in the battles, such as this M-84 ripped open by anti-tank missiles.*

# SERBIAN ARMEI
# IN BOSN

*Above.*
*Pictured in the winter of 1991-92, one of the Serbian Special Forces units tasked with intervening in the 'hot spots' around Sarajevo. To make up for lack of manpower, Serbian Command often calls on such units when vital positions are threatened. The team is equipped with a M-50/70 Praga armoured vehicle, fitted with a 30mm twin gun and a .50 heavy machine-gun.*

On 4 May 1992, Belgrade ordered the Federal forces out of Bosnia Herzegovina. The move was completed within two weeks but all the heavy armament and ammunition depots had been handed over to the militias.

In fact, only 14,000 men, mostly conscripts, had withdrawn from Bosnia. Since then, the Serbian government has always denied any involvement with local Serbian units and stated that no armament or ammunition was ever delivered to them!

Desperately short of weapons, the Bosnian forces surrounded the JNA barracks. All over the country, military operations were afoot and as Croatian forces sneaked into Herzegovina, the Serbs tried to establish direct land communications between all predominently Serbian regions.

*Below.
In Sarajevo, a Serbian
militiaman takes aim with his
assault rifle. His trench is
less than 100m away from the
enemy positions. Although
better equipped, the Serbs
suffered from a dire shortage
of manpower.*

# FORCES

Renamed the Territorial Defence Forces of the Serbian Republic of Bosnia Herzegovina, the Serbian forces were composed of ex-Federal Army units, Serbian militias and para-military formations (responsible for most of the massacres perpetrated in Croatia).

Their first offensive succeeded when they won the battle of Kupres and severed the roads linking central Bosnia to the

Above.
*Ready to defend his home, this Serbian volunteer is on guard duty near the airport in the suburb of Ilidza. He is armed with an M-59/66A1 7.62mm assault rifle, the locally-made version of the Soviet Simonov.*

Dalmatian coast. During the bitter fighting in April, Belgrade openly threw in ex-Federal Army armoured units and engaged them against the Croats defending a strategic plateau in western Herzegovina.

Devoid of support and practically cut off from their rear echelon, the defenders were crushed and the Serbs secured the Sarajevo-Split axis.

Further south, the Serbs spared no effort to capture the bridges on the Neretva river and fighting lasted for several weeks. The town of Mostar, the linchpin of the Serbian positions, was recaptured by the Croats but laid waste in the attack. At the end of March 1993, Mostar was still being shelled by the Serbian heavy guns firing from positions located less than 20km away.

Military activities escalated in the spring of 1992 with the Serbs striking in eastern Bosnia and seizing the main crossing points on the Drina river that marks the border with Serbia. The capture of these

*Pictured in the suburb of Grbavica during the autumn of 1991, a camouflage clad Serbian militiaman ignores the snipers' bullets to give the 'three fingers up' victory sign. Like other parts of the city, this suburb was recaptured after fierce fighting and is reminiscent of Beirut, with its 'green line', snipers and surprise shelling.*

objectives enabled the Serbs to keep supplies flowing steadily to the zones under their control, and to cut off all communications between the Bosnian and Sandjak Muslims.

Bitter fighting resulted when the Serbs struggled to hold the corridor in northern Bosnia, opened to establish an uninterrupted supply line linking Serbia, Krajina and the predominently Serbian region of Banja Luka. To carve out a path through the Croatian and Muslim zones, the Serbs fought bitterly in Derventa, Bosanski Brod, and around Brcko and Gradacac.

In June, the territories allocated to each ethnic group were already outlined, with the Serbs controlling eastern and north-western Bosnia.

From then on, the Serbs would go to any length to retain their territorial gains, and would even agree to a ceasefire, hoping that a UN deployment between the protagonists would help endorse 'Greater Serbia's' new borders.

*Right.*
After firing a salvo of 100mm shells at targets in Sarajevo, Serbian troops survey the result of their shelling. Aware that their adversary has no anti-tank weapons, the Serbs can operate with impunity and need no cover.

*Below.*
Elements of the Serbian forces besieging Sarajevo pictured at the end of the winter of 1992-93. Unlike their Muslim foes who are critically short of heavy equipment and must constantly improvise, the Serbs are well equipped and have plentiful supplies of ammunition.

# THE BESIEGERS OF SARAJEVO

*Far right.*
To shelter Grbavica in Sarajevo's inner city from snipers' fire, the Serbs have built a protection wall with blocks and wrecked buses. Running for several kilometres, this wall is a reminder that the Serbs too are exposed to dangers, as are the Muslims living in the opposite part of the town.

Located in a natural bowl, Sarajevo is easily dominated by an attacker and by the spring of 1992, the Serbs had quickly taken control of most of the hills surrounding the Bosnian capital city.

With the assistance of the Federal Army, the Serbs created several defence lines consisting of infantry positions, artillery batteries and dug-in tanks. Whenever the Bosnians tried to dislodge them, they were beaten back with severe losses as they had no heavy armament to back them up.

The Serbian forces besieging Sarajevo numbered about 3-5,000 men. Their heavy weapons included about 50 T-54/55s, and just as many APCs, supported by 50 130mm and 155mm guns. They also had 100 heavy mortars and plentiful ammunition.

This crushing superiority enabled the besiegers to control the situation and smother any Bosnian counter-attack in a deluge of steel and blood. In the autum of 1992, a Bosnian offensive launched from the Otes suburb was crushed in a

matter of days.

UN observers estimated that the hourly rate of Serbian artillery fire exceeded 1,500 shells. After beating back the Bosnians, the Serbs breached their front line and captured Otes.

During the long siege, Serbian artillerymen fired at Sarajevo over open sights. From the inner Grbavica suburb at the extreme end of the Muslim lines, snipers helped the artillerymen correct the range of their guns.

But Grbavica too had to be protected and a 3km long wall had to be built to shelter Serbian inhabitants from Bosnian snipers. Sarajevo however had more political than strategic significance as the supply routes in the east and in the south-east were already controlled by the Serbs.

A capital city held hostage, Sarajevo should prove a valuable asset during cease-fire negotiations.

# THE SIEGE OF S

The inhabitants of Sarajevo must adjust to the rhythm of the bombings and have to run wherever they go. Even during lulls, they are exposed to fire from snipers or drunken artillerymen who decide to lob a few shells at the besieged city.

On 1 March 1992, the death of a Serb attending a wedding in the Muslim quarter of Sarajevo triggered off a series of violent clashes. This gave the Serbs the pretext they needed to express their staunch opposition to Bosnian independence and in no time, their militias erected barricades across all the access roads to the capital city. The siege began and within a month, Sarajevo was split into two sectors respectively controlled by the Bosnians who defended their stronghold and the Serbs who occupied the outer city. The artillery of the Serbian Republic of Bosnia enforced the blockade by pounding the Muslim quarters and the strategic sites.

The airlift initiated on 29 June did little to help the 350,000 inhabitants. They had had to adjust to terrifying new living conditions. For them, there no longer was such a thing as a safe place: their daily grind was fraught with danger. They had to get used to running through high risk streets, and looking for the tell-tale 'Pazir Snajper' panels (Danger snipers) whenever they queued up for deliveries of bread or water. This hard-

ship came on top of the trauma of dodging the shells lobbed regularly at the city from the Serbian-held, surrounding hills.

In Sarajevo, the atmosphere grew bleaker and bleaker during the grim winter months when each family - deprived of water and electricity - had to constantly reorganise their lodgings to keep out of the snipers' field of fire. Death lurked everywhere and the long, wide avenues like the Proletarian Brigade Boulevard (since nicknamed Sniper Alley) turned into death traps and were never used.

Hope of foreign intervention quickly faded away, and embattled Sarajevo withdrew into itself, grieving at UN helplessness to guarantee even free access to the airport (The Blue Helmets have to get permission from the Serbs whenever a relief convoy crosses their lines).

Long before the winter of 1993 was over, the inhabitants of Sarajevo knew that, apart from bags and crates adorned with the UN logo, they could not expect any military relief, and that the end of the terrible siege was not yet within forseeable sight.

*Right and far right.*
**Sarajevo under fire.**

## THE SIEGE OF SARAJEVO

Bosnian-held areas

Serbian-held areas

UN controlled zones

« "Snipers alley"

Serbian artillery pieces

Towards Belgrade

Towards Belgrade

Hrib

Bistrik

Government house

Grbavica

Dobrinja

Lukavica

Old JNA Barracks

Ilidza

Otes

Stup

Vratnik

Bascarsija

Old Town

Bjevave

Presidential Building

HCR Stores

Zuc

Vogosca

# THE DEFENDERS OF SARAJEVO

The youths of Sarajevo created numerous local militias when the first clashes took place there in March 1992. With names such as the 'Bosnian Patriots', sporting the white lily on their mismatched uniforms, or the 'Serbian Self-Defence League', all these militias were adequately armed. The Serbs were supported by the JNA and, within a few weeks, the 'front line' was defined with long bursts of assault rifles. One month later, tanks and artillery pieces appeared on the Serbian side. Meanwhile, the three large army barracks in Sarajevo had been besieged, stormed and sacked. Officially operating as separate units when the Bosnian Home Ministry split, Bosnian and Serbian police patrols soon vanished from the streets.

In the winter of 1992, Sarajevo's home defence amounted to less than 3,000 new Bosnian Territorial Guard members. These were supported by a few hundred elements of dubious allegiance, armed with Kalashnikovs and entrusted with the defence of a street or a block of houses. In October, Sarajevo's Bosnian headquarters (and Armija command), decided to reorganise the defence forces and set up four combat brigades mustering 1,000 men each. The paramilitary units and their chiefs (halfway between 'Rambos' and bandits) were ordered to fall in with the regulars or vanish.

Simultaneously, armament and ammunition were introduced into the embattled city, but never in sufficient quantities to enable the Bosnians to launch any significant attack.

The three tanks the Bosnians had made little difference. Only once, at the end of December, did the Bosnians succeed in wresting a position from the Serbs: Hill 850 at Buc, in the north of Sarajevo. But the attack was costly and the two weeks of combat brought about a heavy toll in human lives.

Hill 850 is still the only high ground in Bosnian hands and from this vantage point, the defenders overlook their martyred city.

*Above.*
*In the opening stages of the war in Bosnia, members of the local territorial forces had to make do with makeshift weapons such as this grenade launcher improvised from a bicycle frame and a truck suspension spring. This contraption can hurl a hand grenade over 100m with reasonable accuracy*

*Right.*
*Often very young and poorly armed, Bosnian territorials were not short on courage and tackled an adversary whose equipment and armament far outstripped theirs. In the early months of the siege, the Bosnians suffered frightful losses when rushing heavily-defended Serbian positions.*

*In the spring of 1992, the UN forces in Croatia were caught in the crossfire between Muslims and Serbs after setting up their headquarters in Sarajevo. In the picture, a Canadian M-113 on strength with the Royal 22e Regiment waits for a lull in the shelling before heading for Serbian-besieged Dobrinj.*

# UN FORCES

# SARAJEVO

The situation in Bosnia Herzegovina worsened in April and, on 15 May, the Security Council of the United Nations called on the protagonists to define the perimeters of a ceasefire and find a political settlement. New York went as far as demanding that 'Federal Forces' be withdrawn from the defunct republic. But the belligerents ignored UN injunctions and fighting flared anew, obliging the UN to relocate UNPROFOR headquarters to a safer zone away from Sarajevo.

In June, the UN adopted Resolution 758 and more than 1,000 Blue Helmets were deployed at Sarajevo Airport. UNPROFOR 2 was sent in to supervise the delivery of aid relief, in support of UNPROFOR 1 which had been on duty in Croatia since spring 1992. On 28 June President François Mitterrand of France paid a surprise visit to Sarajevo, and the next day, two aircraft carrying supplies landed in the beleaguered city. Two months later, the world discovered the Serbian detention camps, and general revulsion

Right.
*February 1993. From the turret of his VAB, a Legionnaire of 2e REP monitors enemy movements in the ruins of Butmir near Sarajevo Airport.*

Below.
*President Mitterrand's visit in July 1992 combined with international pressure led to Sarajevo Airport being reopened and soon, members of 1st Coy, 2e RIMA backed up by Canadian M-113 APCs cleared the runway for traffic. From then on, about 16 relief flights were made daily, undeterred by fire from uncontrolled elements on either side of the runway. Only shelling interrupted the shuttle flights.*

led the UN to protect the convoys delivering humanitarian aid to the Bosnian zones besieged by the Serbs. The Security Council implied that force could be used in case of opposition, and on two occasions, British Blue Helmets implemented the UN decision by opening up at Serbian militiamen with 30mm cannon.

In early September, the relief operation was in full swing. Relief aircraft were plying between Split on the Dalmatian coast and Sarajevo when an Italian G-222 was shot down by a missile. UN involvement increased when relief convoys were given additional protection, and extra troops commanded by the French General Morillon were deployed in Bosnia on 15 October.

For several days, and in compliance with UN Resolution 781, Serbian aircraft had been banned from Bosnian air space but to bypass that order, the Serbs emulated the UN by repainting their aircraft white!

In January 1993, 2,400 Blue Helmets were deployed in Bosnia. Equipped with light 127

*Left.*
*Manning a checkpoint near one of the airport's boundaries, Legionnaires watch as a C-130 Hercules takes off. For the first time in their history, Legionnaires have swapped their green berets for the famous blue headgear of UN forces.*

armour, APCs and artillery pieces, 2,400 British soldiers were stationed there. Numbering 1,400 men, the French battalion was posted around Bihac (north-western Bosnia) with its Sagaie light tanks, 81mm mortars, Milan anti-tank missiles, Gazelle and Puma combat helicopters. The French contingent was bolstered by the 400 Legionnaires from 2e REP who arrived in February 1993 to relieve the 'Marsouins' who had been on duty in and around Sarajevo airport since September 1992.

The rest of the UN deployment in the old Yugoslavia includes: 1,000 Canadian Blue Helmets, 800 Spaniards equipped with armed vehicles and tasked with escorting convoys, 400 Egyptians operating mostly around Sarajevo, 400 Ukrainians, also assigned to the Bosnian capital city, 200 Danes,

and 100 Belgians scattered around the various sectors.

Although the various ethnic minorities in Bosnia resent their presence and accuse them of playing the enemy's game, the Blue Helmets continuously prove their worth during emergencies or when they see the humanitarian convoys safely through to their final destinations. But the price they have paid in Bosnia is heavy: by February 1993, 20 had laid down their lives in ambushes or clashes initiated by parties willing to force western powers to intervene or to keep the Blue Helmets away from the slaughter. However, it wasn't until 19 February 1993 that the UN soldiers were authorised to return fire if attacked.

Until then, they were nothing but defenceless targets.

*Right.*
*In summer 1992 UN convoys were often fired at by Serbian or Muslim snipers as they supplied the Blue Helmets and delivered relief to the population. This fire was often deliberate and aimed at disrupting the work of the UN. In the picture, Canadian vehicles and elements from French GSL (Logistic Support) are under fire from a Serbian heavy machine-gun.*

*Left.*
*In July 1992 at Sarajevo Airport, 'Marsouins' of 2e RIMa manning checkpoint 'Romeo' observe the shelling of Bosnian and Croatian positions. Although they had no heavy weapons, 'Marsouins' and French Marine Commandos withstood Serbian pressure until their deployment was officially endorsed by the UN.*

*Right.*
*In February 1993, UN officers with VABs from 1st Coy, 2e REP conduct a reconnaissance on the outskirts of the airport to check the protection fence. Every night, fighters and civilians risked their lives when they crossed the asphalt to reach Croatian-held zones.*

# UN FORCES IN

*Right.*
*The assignments of UN forces in Bosnia differ to those of their counterparts in Croatia, as they must escort relief convoys through the combat zones. UN forces in Croatia are allowed to return fire if they come under attack but often their convoys find themselves immobilised by lack of firmness from the Security Council or European governments - and also by the ill will of the Serbs who resent the UN supplying their enemy. In 1993, a French VAB protects a UN transport vehicle bringing in supplies to a Muslim zone near Sarajevo, now almost entirely surrounded by the Serbs.*

*Below.*
*An M-113 APC of Royal 22e Regiment in position in Bosnia. In the early stages of the war, UN vehicles could easily cross the front lines. Along with the French, the British, the Danes, the Spaniards and the Canadians are entrusted with the most dangerous assignments.*

*Right.* **A Ukrainian BTR-70 APC patrolling through the outskirts of the Bosnian capital city. In the early stages of the deployment, these soldiers were often fired at by Serbian artillerymen until UN command authorised the Blue Helmets to fire back when attacked. Shelling soon stopped when the UN soldiers opened up with .50 heavy machine-guns at whatever Serbian snipers or soldiers had been spotted.**

*Following pages.* **Codenamed Operation 'Grapple', the British deployment in Bosnia began in October 1992 and involved more than 2,300 soldiers with their heavy equipment. Based in the centre of the country, the British escorted humanitarian convoys and did not hesitate to fire the 30mm cannon of their Warriors whenever they came under Serbian fire. The elements shown here belong to British Battalion Group 68, and are armed with 30mm cannon.**

131

# THE BATTALION OF HOPE

*Above.*
*French Blue Helmets of the UNPROFOR deployment in Krajina survey ruined buildings in September 1992. Gradually, the French won the confidence of the belligerents and achieved their missions: demilitarising the front line to a depth of 20km, and seeing the relief convoys through safely, especially to the Bihac pocket.*

During the winter of 1992-93, the French Blue Helmets were the only hope and link with the outside world for the population of Bihac. Only the presence of the French Battalion (French Bat. 3) in this enclave enabled 300,000 people to survive.

When it was deployed in Bihac in the autumn of 1992, French Bat. 3 numbered 1,250 officers, NCOs and rank and file soldiers (60% of whom were volunteer conscripts).

Equipped with about 430 vehicles and 19 Sagaie light tanks, the Battalion stretched over 37km as it filed through the Serbian lines and into the town of Velika-Kladusa after a 10-hour journey.

To the fury of the Serbs, the French took up position in the heartland of the Muslim enclave where they were greeted rapturously by the locals whose welcome verged on delirium.

When deployed in February 1993, the 1,400-man strong Battalion was commanded by Colonel Dresse, and was composed of regiments levied from the 15e Division d'Infanterie and from elements supplied by the France's FAR (Rapid Reaction Force).

The ERC-90 light tank squadron was supplied by Angoulême 1e RIMa, and the specialised units were provided by 2e Corps d'Armée. The Battalion also included a light aviation detachment and a forward surgical unit.

Thanks to the composure of its soldiers and the determination of its command, the French Battalion escorted 50 relief trucks a week instead of the five originally scheduled.

But even more important than relief, the French Battalion restored hope to Bihac.

*Above.*
**December 1992. An armoured column of British Blue Helmets of 42nd Field Squadron, the Royal Engineers, about to leave their base at Vitez in the heartland of Bosnia. The British conducted most of their missions from there, and were mainly involved with escorting and protecting relief convoys.**

*Right.*
**A symbol of peace: a blue beret on a British vehicle. The UN presence in Bosnia was a major step towards peace and made the delivery of aid relief to the population possible.**

135

*Right.*
*In February 1993, the crew of a Croatian Model 55 (Soviet Model 39) 30mm anti-aircraft gun are ready to repel any air attack the Serbs may launch at southern Croatia, Maslenica and Zemunik airport. Although the Serbs shelled the city of Zadar on the Dalmatian coast, they never regained the lost ground.*

# WAR FLARES A

*Right.*
*These members of a Croatian territorial brigade give the victory sign as they defend the front line against Serbian militia in Krajina. In spite of their superior armament - they recovered all the heavy armament impounded from them by the UN - the Serbs could not stem the major offensive the Croats launched in January 1993.*

*Below.*
*Formerly on strength with the JNA, this M-84 MBT was knocked out in the vicinity of Zadar during the winter of 1992-93. During this engagement, the Serbs lost many tanks and APCs, even though the ground afforded scant protection to the Croats.*

# AIN IN CROATIA

Backed up by heavy artillery and several multiple rocket launchers, Croatian forces struck towards the Dalmatian coast on 22 January 1993. Their main objectives were the famous Maslenica bridge, Zadar's Zemunik airport and the Peruca dam. Taken by surprise, the Serbs were gradually pushed back and their front line was eventually breached.

Fighting was bitter and villages changed hands several times. Two French Blue Helmets were killed and another two wounded in the opening moves of the offensive. For the first time in 18 months, Zadar was shelled again.

The Serbs rushed reinforcements to Knin and dozens of volunteers flocked to the recruiting centres all over Serbia. The whole region was placed on full alert as strong Croatian concentrations had been reported to the south of Drnis.

With dismay, the UN realised that several months of effort had been wiped out as the Croatian move nullified any prospects of an international intervention against the Serbs in Bosnia.

From then on, the Serbs could no longer be regarded as the only aggressors, and the Security Council asked President Tudjman to withdraw his forces back to the ceasefire line.

The Croatian leader stated that unlike the UN, he had been able to implement the Vance-Owen Plan and that Croatia had to recapture the Maslenica bridge, absolutely vital to its interests. But the Vance-Owen Plan had only been partially enforced: the refugees had not been repatriated and although the Serbian militiamen had been disarmed, most had simply swapped their camouflage for police uniforms.

This untimely Croatian offensive marked another turning point in the war as, from then on, the Serbian heavy weapons no longer were decisive.

For the first time since World War 2, two conventional armies were opposed on European soil.

*Above.*
*The ruins of the famous Maslenica bridge as they appeared in February 1993. Providing a vital link between northern Dalmatia and the coast, this bridge was blown up in the autumn of 1991 just before it fell into Serbian hands . After endless negotiations conducted under UN auspices, the Serbs grudgingly agreed to hand over whatever was left of the bridge to the Croats before the end of 1992, but when the Serbs failed to keep their word, Croatian forces attacked and recaptured the bridge in January 1993.*

*Right.*
*In a firing position on the island of Pag, in the vicinity of Zadar, a Croatian BRDM-2 armed with an SA-9 Gaskin anti-aircaft missile launcher defending one of the vital bridges linking the towns of southern Croatia. In autumn 1991, the Croats retrieved many vehicles of this type from the JNA barracks.*

*An A-6E Intruder aircraft about to take off from the deck of aircraft carrier USS J. F. Kennedy. Bosnian airspace has now been declared a no-fly zone by a UN resolution and aircraft of western nations may now intervene to enforce this decision. The UN however, has yet to decide whether these aircraft may engage in combat with Serbian aircraft and bomb ground facilities such as runways, shelters and anti-air defence poisitions.*

# TOWARDS WESTE

The days when the major powers were ready to go to war over Sarajevo are now well and truly over even though their leaders are aware that the conflict may spread beyond its current borders. They still hope that the war will remain within its confines and eventually die out, inevitably bringing about the dismemberment of the still-born Bosnian-Herzegovinian Republic.

Sadly, it seems that neither the massive deployment of 15,000 Blue Helmets from 25 nations in Serbian-occupied territories, nor the intervention of a further 9,000 in Bosnia have achieved anything. The UN forces couldn't stop the war and did not prevent the Serbian militias and the Croatian army from fighting it out again on the Dalmatian coast. The UN also failed to guarantee the free movement of relief convoys through Bosnian territory, and could not implement the repatriation of refugees as

# N INTERVENTION?

specified in the Vance-Owen Plan. Cashing in on the weariness of western nations and hoping that they will acknowledge a *fait accompli*, the Serbs feel strong enough to ignore UN resolutions. Albeit an EEC member, Greece defies the embargo decreed against Serbia, and along with its neighbours, took no heed of the sanctions imposed by the UN.

As time passes, humanitarian operations gradually give way to armed intervention and the UN forces reluctantly find themselves increasingly committed to peace keeping.

At the end of winter 1993, the possibility of a 'Desert Storm' operation in the Balkans seemed remote, as the three larger powers were afraid of getting bogged down in a region devoid of strategic significance. In August 1992, western leaders rejected the possibility of intervening as they did in Kuwait, for neither the Americans nor the Europeans were willing to

*Left.*
*During the winter 1992-93, France deployed her aircraft carrier* Clemenceau *and a sizeable support fleet in the Adriatic. With the US Navy, the Royal Navy and other NATO naval forces, the French may launch air strikes at Serbian air bases and strategic points in Bosnia, or bomb Serbian-held zones in Croatia.*

send troops into the Balkan quagmire. The British refused to pay the price in blood; as for the French, they consider that sending infantry forces into such rugged terrain would be a costly mistake. For their part, the Americans would favour the safety of air strikes launched from a carrier force in the Adriatic. But aware that their Blue Helmets would become the prime targets of all the protagonists if the Americans had things their way, the Europeans rejected the US proposal.

A political solution after a ceasefire was the only course of action acceptable to western leaders - even though this would only endorse the Serbs' conquests and result in the Mus-

lims losing their best land. Inevitably, they would end up in the poorest areas which, in the long term, would turn them into Europe's Palestinians. Such a course of action could also result in a stalemate. Only military intervention can prevent another Munich and the political capitulation that could result in war spreading to Albania, Bulgaria, Greece, Macedonia, Romania, and Turkey.

So how can the catastrophe that led to World War 1 be prevented from repeating itself? And how can a Munich-style of capitulation be avoided?

The answer may lie in the snow-capped mountains of Bosnia...

142

*Right.*
*Legionnaires of 2e REI storming a town during an urban fighting exercise in southern France. Could this be a foretaste of the liberation of Sarajevo? Even though peace had been restored on the Bosnian front by the end of 1992, the offensives launched by the Croats in January 1993 and by the Serbs in spring 1993 showed how powerless UN forces were, and that the Blue Helmets could do little more than take punishment before withdrawing from the front line with their dead and wounded. Any massive operation against the Serbs in Bosnia would certainly result in heavy losses. Are the western powers prepared to pay the price?*

# ACKNOWLEDGEMENTS

The authors wish to thank particularly the fighters who protected them during their assignments, as well as the *French Army's Public Relations Office*, the *British Army's Public Relations Office*, and the *UN Public Relations Office*. We also wish to extend our gratitude to Mr *Dalo* who never objected to hiring us cars, irrespective of the perilous areas we would drive them to.

# PHOTO CREDITS

**Eric MICHELETTI :** 1, 6, 7, 8, 10, 11, 12, 13, 14, 15, 16, 17, 18, 19, 23 *(bottom)*,24, 25, 32, 33,36, 37 ,40 *(bottom)*, 41, 42, 43, 44 *(top)*,45, 46, 54, 55 *(top)*, 72 *(top)*, 88, 89,96, 97 *(top)*, 101, 132, 133, 135,

**Yves DEBAY :** 4, 9, 20, 21,22, 23 *(top)* 26, 28, 29,38, 39, 40 *(top)*,44, 47, 48, 49, 50, 51, 52, 53, 55 *(bottom)*, 56, 57, 58, 59,60, 61, 66, 68, 69, 70, 71,72 *(bottom)*, 73, 74, 75,76, 77, 78, 79, 80, 82, 83, 84, 85, 86, 90, 92, 93, 94, 95, 97*(bottom)*, 98, 100, 102, 103, 104, 105, 107,108, 109, 110, 111, 112, 113, 116, 117, 118, 120, 121, 122, 123, 124, 126, 127, 128, 129, 130, 131, 134, 136, 137, 138, 139, 140, 142, 143 .

**Jean-Philippe DALLIES :** 145 *(left)*

Design: Jean-Marie MONGIN, Eric MICHELETTI
Maps: Stéphane BALLE and Jean-Marie MONGIN © PLST
We also wish to thank Alexandra GARDINER for her invaluable assistance.

ISBN: *2 908 182 211*
Publisher's number: *2-908182*
Published by **Histoire & Collections**
19, avenue de la République, 7511
Paris, France
Tel.: International *(1) 43.57.83.83*
Fax: International *(1) 40.21.97.55*

Editorial composition: *McIntosh II FX, X-Press and Adobe Illustrator.*

Photography: *SCIPE, Paris*

Colour separation: *Ozaland, Paris.*

Printed by *SIB* of Saint-Léonard, France, on 31 May 1993.